TWAYNE'S WORLD AUTHORS SERIES

A Survey of the World's Literature

Sylvia E. Bowman, Indiana University

GENERAL EDITOR

NORWAY

Leif Sjöberg, State University of New York, Stony Brook

EDITOR

Sigrid Undset

(TWAS 107)

TWAYNE'S WORLD AUTHORS SERIES (TWAS)

*The purpose of TWAS is to survey the major writers
—novelists, dramatists, historians, poets, philosophers,
and critics—of the nations of the world. Among the
national literatures covered are those of Australia,
Canada, China, Eastern Europe, France, Germany,
Greece, India, Italy, Japan, Latin America, New Zea-
land, Poland, Russia, Scandinavia, Spain, and the
African nations, as well as Hebrew, Yiddish, and
Latin Classical literatures. This survey is comple-
mented by Twayne's United States Authors Series
and English Authors Series.*

*The intent of each volume in these series is to present
a critical-analytical study of the works of the writer;
to include biographical and historical material that
may be necessary for understanding, appreciation,
and critical appraisal of the writer; and to present all
material in clear, concise English—but not to vitiate
the scholarly content of the work by doing so.*

Sigrid Undset

By CARL F. BAYERSCHMIDT

Columbia University

Twayne Publishers, Inc.   ::   New York

TO DOROTHY

To Dorothy

Preface

During the third and fourth decades of the twentieth century Sigrid Undset was acclaimed as one of the greatest realistic writers of the time. Other than the poet and dramatist Henrik Ibsen (1828–1906) and the composer Edvard Grieg (1843–1907) no Norwegian enjoyed such international fame as this gifted novelist. Her two medieval epics, *Kristin Lavransdatter* and *Olav Audunssön*, were translated into foreign languages and became bestsellers almost immediately in Denmark, Sweden, Finland, Latvia, Poland, Russia, Holland, France, Czechoslovakia, Hungary, Italy, Spain, Portugal, and particularly in Germany, England, and the United States.

After mid-century, however, interest in Sigrid Undset's works seemed to taper off somewhat, although in her homeland she continued to be recognized as her country's greatest woman writer. It was the contention of some critics that her later works are tendentious and contain too much Catholic propaganda. It is true that some of these works, particularly *The Wild Orchid* and *The Burning Bush* as well as some of her essays have a special appeal to Catholic readers, but she is never inflexible in her defense of Catholic doctrine, for she writes as a Christian who emphasizes the empirical rather than the dogmatic side of religion. Indeed, it is her liberal attitude toward all religious belief that has particular relevance to the ecumenicity of our own day and age and contributes in no small measure to the enduring value of her entire literary production.

Sigrid Undset practices an active faith in God and believes in the indomitable realism of the Church. She stresses fundamental truths which cannot be evaded today any more easily than they could be in the past. She is a stern and severe moralist, but at the same time she reveals sympathy and understanding for men and women who live below their potential and fall into error, for she is realistic enough not to expect perfection on earth. Honesty and truthfulness are the watchwords of all her writing. For this reason she does not portray people as they should be, but as they are, and this she does with neither a smile of approval nor with a scowl of reproach, for judgment does not lie in her hands.

To her mastery of background material and historical detail Sigrid Undset adds a penetrating psychological insight into the mentality and character of modern and bygone times. The men and women of her novels are creatures of flesh and blood; they come alive before us so that we can understand them and believe in them. It is because Sigrid Undset combines art and life to such a degree of perfection that she must be considered one of the great novelists of all time and certainly Scandinavia's most outstanding woman writer.

Biographical material about Sigrid Undset is not too plentiful. Except for her own childhood reminiscences, *The Longest Years,* and the account she gives of her flight from Norway and stay in America in *Return to the Future* Sigrid Undset has written very little about herself. It is fortunate, therefore, that Nini Roll Anker has written of her friendship with the author in her charming account *Min venn Sigrid Undset.* Also of particular help in this study has been Professor A. H. Winsnes' excellent book which has been translated from Norwegian into English by P. G. Foote as *Sigrid Undset: A Study in Christian Realism.* I am grateful to Sheed and Ward, Inc., publishers of this translation, for permission to quote several passages from it.

I should also like to express my sincere gratitude to Mrs. Signe Undset Thomas, a younger sister of Sigrid Undset, and to Mrs. Borghild Helland-Hansen, a friend since childhood of the Undset family. Both these ladies living in Oslo have given me many interesting bits of information about Norway's great writer. I am also indebted to Mr. Carl F. Engelstad, literary editor of the *Aftenposten* in Oslo and author of an excellent study on Sigrid Undset's medieval novels. To him as well as to Ebba Haslund (Mrs. Sverre Halvorsen) and Pater H. Rieber-Mohn O.P., likewise of Oslo, go my sincere thanks for their many helpful suggestions which I have been able to include in this study.

I am also very grateful to Professor Helen M. Mustard of Columbia University and to Sister Margaret Mary Dunn of Barat College of the Sacred Heart for reading the original manuscript

Preface

and making many improvements in factual and stylistic matters. Above all I owe thanks to Professor Leif Sjöberg of the State University of New York at Stony Brook and to Mr. Erik J. Friis, editor of The American-Scandinavian Foundation. Both have been of invaluable help to me in making available much bibliographical material and for their constant advice and guidance in the preparation of the manuscript.

C.F.B.

New York
March 1969

Contents

Contents

Chronology

1882   May 20, Sigrid Undset born in Kalundborg, a city in the western part of Sjælland, Denmark, as the eldest of three daughters of Ingvald and Anna Charlotte Undset.

1884   Family moved to Christiania (Oslo).

1893   December, father died.

1898   Graduated from Commercial College.

1899–   Ten years of office employment in Oslo.
1909

1905   Norway severed the union with Sweden.

1907   Published the novel *Fru Marta Oulie* (*Mrs. Marta Oulie*).

1908   Published the collection of short stories, *Den lykkelige alder* (*The Happy Age*) and a one-act play, *I graalysningen* (*In the Gray Light of Dawn*).

1909   Published a tale in saga style, *Fortellingen om Viga-Ljot og Vigdis* (*Gunnar's Daughter*).

1909–   Received scholarship for study in Italy. Also visited Paris
1910   and then returned to Oslo in autumn of 1910. Became acquainted with author Nini Roll Anker. Published collection of poems, *Ungdom* (*Youth*).

1911   Published the novel *Jenny*.

1912   Married artist Anders C. Svarstad in Antwerp and lived in Hammersmith, London. Published the collection of short stories *Fattige skjebner* (*Poor Fortunes*).

1912–   Lived in Rome from December, 1912, to April, 1913. First
1913   son, Anders, born in Rome, January 12, 1913. Returned to Oslo.

1913–   Lived at Ski, near Oslo, from July, 1913, to the summer
1916   of 1916.

1914   March, delivered an address, "Det fjerde bud" ("The Fourth Commandment"), in Students' Union, Oslo. Published the novel *Vaaren* (*Spring*).

1915 Published *Fortellinger om Kong Artur og ridderne av det runde bord* (*Tales of King Arthur and the Knights of the Round Table*). Daughter, Maren Charlotte, born at Ski, October 29.

1916– Lived at East Aker.
1919

1917 Spent summer months at Laurgaard in Sel (Gudbrandsdal). Published two short stories in *Splinten av troldspeilet* (*Images in a Mirror*).

1918 Published the collection of short stories *De kloge jomfruer* (*The Wise Virgins*).

1919 Summer, moved to Lillehammer, where she lived until April, 1940. Published the collection of essays *Et kvindesynspunkt* (*A Woman's Point of View*). Third child, Hans, born at Lillehammer.

1920 Purchased "Bjerkebæk," her home at Lillehammer. Published the novel *Kransen* (*The Bridal Wreath*), first part of *Kristin Lavransdatter*.

1921 Published the novel *Husfrue* (*The Mistress of Husaby*), second part of *Kristin Lavransdatter*.

1922 Published the novel *Korset* (*The Cross*), third part of *Kristin Lavransdatter*.

1923 Published her translation *Tre sagaer om islændinger* (*Three Sagas of Icelanders*).

1924 November 24, converted to Catholicism in parish church at Hamar; marriage to Svarstad annulled.

1925 Spent Easter at Monte Cassino, Italy, with mother and son Anders. Published the narrative *Sankt Halvards liv, död og jertegn* (*Saint Halvard's Life, Death and Miracles*) and the novel *Olav Audunssön i Hestviken* (*Olav Audunssön of Hestviken*).

1927 Published the essay "Katholsk propaganda" ("Catholic Propaganda") and the novel *Olav Audunssön og hans börn* (*Olav Audunssön and His Children*).

1928 Nobel Prize for Literature awarded. Donated 15,000 Norwegian crowns to the Norwegian Authors' Association.

1929 Published the collection of essays *Etapper* (*Stages on the Road*) and the novel *Gymnadenia* (*The Wild Orchid*).

1930 Published the novel *Den brennende busk* (*The Burning Bush*), the historical narrative *Hellig Olav, Norges konge*

(*Saint Olav, King of Norway*) and a meditation, *Das Weihnachtswunder* (*The Miracle of Christmas*).

1931 Published a collection of essays, *Begegnungen und Trennungen* (*Meeting and Parting*).

1932 Published the novel *Ida Elisabeth*, and a collection of reflections, *Christmas and Twelfth Night*.

1933 Published the collection of essays *Etapper. Ny række* (*Stages on the Road*).

1934 Published the autobiographical reminiscences *Elleve aar* (*The Longest Years*).

1935 Published the essay "Fortschritt, Rasse, Religion" ("Progress, Race, Religion"). Attended meeting of Scandinavian authors in Helsinki.

1936 Published the novel *Den trofaste hustru* (*The Faithful Wife*). Works eliminated from libraries in Germany.

1937 Published a historical and legendary narrative, *Norske helgener* (*Saga of Saints*).

1938 Published a collection of essays, *Selvportretter og landskapsbilleder* (*Men, Women and Places*).

1939 Published the novel *Madame Dorthea*.

1940 April 6, delivered an address entitled "Christianity and Our Time" in Students' Union in Oslo. April 20, fled from Lillehammer and arrived in Sweden where she learned of death of son Anders on April 26 while serving with ambulance unit in Norway. July 14, left Sweden and journeyed through Russia and Siberia to Japan, and then arriving in San Francisco on August 26. Books destroyed by Nazis in Norway. Donated Nobel Prize gold medal for aid to Finns.

1940– Lived in New York and traveled in the United States. Be-
1945 came acquainted with Willa Cather and Marjorie Kinnan Rawlings.

1942 Published recollections in *Tilbake til fremtiden* (*Return to the Future*) and *Happy Times in Norway*. Honorary degree conferred by Rollins College.

1943 Published the children's tale *Sigurd and His Brave Companions*. Honorary degree conferred by Smith College.

1945 Published the collection of tales *True and Untrue and Other Norse Tales*. August, returned to Lillehammer.

1947 On birthday, May 20, Grand Cross of the Order of Saint Olav conferred by King Haakon VII of Norway.

1949 June 10, Sigrid Undset died at Lillehammer.
1951 Posthumous publication of the biography *Caterina av Siena* (*Catherine of Siena*).
1952 A. H. Winsnes published her articles and speeches from the war years in *Artikler og taler fra krigstiden.*

Introduction

SIGRID UNDSET (1882–1949) was awarded the Nobel Prize
for Literature in 1928, principally for her powerful pictures
of life in medieval Norway. She reached the peak of her creative
artistry in her two novels of thirteenth- and fourteenth-century
Norway, *Kristin Lavransdatter* (1920–22) and *Olav Audunssön*
(1925–27), for it was this period in Scandinavian history which
had fascinated her from earliest youth. Her remark, "I have lived
for two thousand years in this country," expresses her undying
love for her native land and her feeling of spiritual kinship with
all ages from the time of St. Augustine in the fourth and fifth
centuries to the contemporary world of King Haakon VII.

There is a timeless quality to all of Sigrid Undset's work because of her feeling for the continuity of historical development.
The characters that emerge so lifelike from the pages of her novels are all part of common humanity, whether they live in Viking
times, in the Middle Ages, or in twentieth-century Norway. Her
works are part of a tradition of realistic writing which first appeared in Norwegian letters around 1870, although her first novel,
Mrs. Marta Oulie, was not published until 1907.

Unlike most of her older contemporaries Sigrid Undset did not
become involved in any program of social or political reform. She
was fully aware of the controversies and agitations that stirred
most minds in the early years of the twentieth century, but she
preferred to maintain a position of restrained detachment. In her
works one finds scarcely an echo of the events which led up to
Norway's severance of the union with Sweden in 1905. Much
more significant to her were the people whose lives were played
out upon the canvas of those changing times. Like Knut Hamsun
she believed that literature should reflect the unconscious life of
the soul. At the conclusion of her *Tales of King Arthur and the*

17

Knights of the Round Table (1915) she writes: "Manners and customs are constantly changing. People's beliefs are likewise altered and they think differently about many things, but the human heart does not change in the least through all ages."

It is this human heart in all its spiritual and emotional conflicts with which Sigrid Undset was concerned. Her moral convictions are formulated according to fundamental conservative principles tested by time. These truths, which distinguish sharply between right and wrong, seemed to her best exemplified in the human relationships that find expression in family and home, between husband and wife, between parents and children. The individual, moreover, must also establish a proper contact with society, for his actions can be judged solely on the basis of such a relationship. Of utmost importance therefore is the sense of responsibility which he must feel toward his fellow man, and the greater the talents that have been bestowed upon him the greater this responsibility must be. To withdraw into the narrow circle of one's own ego is to lose one of the most basic values of a purposeful life, the capacity for loyalty to something greater than oneself.

Sigrid Undset's deep religious faith is reflected in her works even before her conversion to Catholicism in 1924. Although she had considered herself an agnostic in her youth, her instinctive religious sensibility had enabled her to feel a profound reverence for all that is sacred in human experience. Even the old pagans who made offerings to their gods were aware of some divine order to which they owed obedience and on which their lives depended. The modern pagans, however, worship other gods. Their materialistic outlook on life is a reflection of their egocentric individualism. Many of their self-created ideas are hostile to the recognition of a supernatural reality.

She was equally opposed to all political doctrines and collective movements that repudiate Christianity as the greatest obstacle to the realization of their programs. In Communism, Fascism, and Nazism she recognized forces which would deny man the freedom of his soul and his intrinsic worth in the world of the spirit.

In her search for truth Sigrid Undset saw that Christianity possessed an inner logic, the world being an ordinance of divine reason in which God has created man in His own image. One either denies all ultimate values and seeks the law of life within his own small consciousness or one accepts Christianity as a concrete historical fact and seeks to bring one's own will into harmony with the will of God.

Sigrid Undset turned to the Catholic Church because she considered it identical with the Church which Christ had established. She introduced a certain amount of what might be called religious propaganda into her later works, as for example *The Wild Orchid* (1929) and *The Burning Bush* (1930), but for the most part she stressed the empirical rather than the dogmatic side of the Catholic faith.

Carrying on the tradition of Norwegian realistic writers of the nineteenth century, she described the outer world in all truth exactly as she saw it without romantic artificiality. She also probed deeply into the inner lives of her characters and sought to understand their thoughts and actions in relationship to the society in which they lived.

The geographical setting within which life was played out was to her an important growth factor. With a most sensuous perception she was able to describe the Norwegian landscape in all its grandeur and beauty, with its wild forests and rushing streams, its high fells and broad fjords. There are some moments of light and color in her novels, but for the most part she has painted a somber and gray picture of human existence. Her characters, whether they are drawn from the present or the past, are described with such objective truth and keen psychological insight that she must be counted among the greatest realistic writers of the first half of the twentieth century.

Sigrid Undset's realism is neither pessimistic, as is Strindberg's, nor fatalistic, as is Ibsen's. Though the conditions of life imposed on her characters are always difficult, she reveals a compassionate and understanding heart for them as they struggle to discover some meaning and purpose in their lives. This meaning lies in man's assumption of responsibility to his family and his society and, on a metaphysical plane, in his loyalty to his God. The intense brooding and endless hours of anguish in her major works show that in the conflict of conscience it is easy to fall, but difficult to rise again. Nevertheless, Sigrid Undset's basic optimism is expressed in her belief that man has been given the free choice to do God's will and that the channels of grace through which he is prepared for eternity always remain open if he keeps the covenant made with God.

CHAPTER 1

Life

I Childhood and Youth (1882–1899)

SIGRID UNDSET was born on May 20, 1882 in the small Danish town of Kalundborg, the eldest of the three daughters of Ingvald and Anna Charlotte Undset (née Gyth). Her father who came from the Trondheim area of Norway, was a renowned archeologist and the author of a scholarly work on the beginnings of the Iron Age in Northern Europe (1881), a more popular study on the first beginnings of the Oslo Valley (1890) and a book of memoirs entitled *Fra Akershus til Akropolis* (1888–92). Her mother, Anna Charlotte Gyth, daughter of a distinguished chancery councillor of Kalundborg, was only eleven years old when her own mother died and her maiden aunt Signe Dorthea Worsöe came to keep house for the widowed brother-in-law and his six motherless children.

Aunt Signe did her best to spoil Anna Charlotte, the prettiest and most precocious of the six children, and without doubt some of Anna Charlotte's reserve and pride may have been attributed to the favored treatment given her by "Moster" Signe. She was an intelligent child and later became an ideal mate for her learned husband. She took an active interest in his scholarly work and accompanied him on his travels. It was on a research trip to the Mediterranean countries in 1880 that Ingvald Undset suffered an attack of malaria and was forced to return home. The young couple made their home in Kalundborg instead of venturing as far as Trondheim in the north. Here they lived in a wing of the large Empire-style house of the councillor, and it was here in the home of her maternal grandfather that Sigrid Undset was born and where she spent the first two years of her life.

Sigrid Undset has written a fascinating account of her childhood in *Elleve aar* (*The Longest Years*), 1934. She could of course recall little of these first two years, and there is in general an element of "Dichtung und Wahrheit" in this beautifully told autobiographical and psychological study. However, there were frequent visits to Kalundborg during the summer holidays after her family had moved to Christiania (renamed Oslo in 1925), and from her mother's "Moster" Signe, skillful in the art of storytelling, the young girl must have heard so many accounts of the little happenings in these early years that she came to believe that they were part of her own conscious experience. In any case, she felt that she could remember these first years as a "perpetual basking in sunshine on warm earth." [1]

When Sigrid Undset was two years old the family moved to Christiania where Ingvald Undset was associated with the archeological section of the University Museum. During Sigrid Undset's youth her parents had occasion to move from one section of Christiania to another, so that the young girl was able in this way to receive many childhood impressions from all parts of the capital city. Each district of Christiania had its peculiar charm, but probably none quite as much as the delightful Lyder Sagen Street, situated at the outskirts of the city between rural West Aker and the town proper. Sigrid Undset recalls very vividly the four happy years spent here and especially her association with the Winter-Hjelm family ("Wilster," as they are called in *The Longest Years*). The Winter-Hjelms lived on the first floor below the Undsets at 10 Lyder Sagen Street. There were twelve children in the family and all had their own friends. "Uninvited and without any feeling of embarrassment most of the youngsters of the street paraded through the Wilsters' rooms, coming in at the veranda and going out by the back door." [2] To Sigrid the German-born Mrs. Winter-Hjelm was the most beautiful woman in the world, completely unperturbed by the flock of children constantly fluttering about her. In her company the children enjoyed frequent walks through meadows and fields and picnics in the woods where she thrilled them with the retelling of fairy tales of Undine, Rübezahl, Melusine, and many others from her native Germany.

Because of Ingvald Undset's poor health it became necessary for the family to seek new living quarters in the heart of the city, close to the University Museum. The new home on Keyser Street, with its dark cellars and gloomy corridors and with windows facing cheerless courtyards, was in direct contrast to the bright and friendly atmosphere which had prevailed in Lyder Sagen Street,

but the young girl soon found these surroundings just as exciting.
The area around St. Olav's Church, Trinity Church, and the Palace Park she was later to consider the true Christiania, and in her
novels of modern life she has given a very realistic description of
the bustling activity in the streets and shops of this very part of
town. In *The Longest Years* she writes: "She had loved the little
front gardens of the Keyser Street quarter with a sentimental and
fanatical affection for every bush that burst into leaf and every
tuft of daffodil or phlox that sent up its shoots through the crust of
dirty ice—in a way it was a melancholy place to live in, but it had
its comforts, and nowhere was it dull." [3]

By comparison with Keyser Street, which she came to know so
intimately, her new home in Observatory Street, in the western
part of the town, seemed an entirely foreign country. What she
liked least of all about it was the snobbishness of the people,
many of whom preferred to be taken for something they were not.
She was aware of the fact that because of her father's illness her
family had difficulties in making ends meet, but she always accepted this fact as something natural and by no means humiliating.

After her father's death in 1893, the family moved to Steen
Street, where people did not consider it a disgrace to be poor.
Furthermore, she was now once again just a stone's throw away
from her beloved Lyder Sagen Street and was free to roam all
over the hills and valleys of the West Aker region.

Despite the shadow cast by her father's long illness Sigrid Undset's childhood was a happy one. Her mother was devoted to her
three children and was determined to give them a proper upbringing, but she had neither time nor inclination for any display of
affection. The young girl had great respect for her mother, but at
the same time she recognized her impulsiveness as well as the
rigidity of her likes and dislikes. There were strong bonds of affection, however, between Sigrid and her father, and it was not without reason that she gave herself the name Ingvild in *The Longest
Years*. In the figure of Lavrans in her medieval novel *Kristin Lavransdatter*, Sigrid Undset was later to pay a stirring tribute to the
memory of her father. [4]

With fond memories she also recalled the summers spent either
in Kalundborg with her grandfather and great-aunt Signe or in
Trondheim with her paternal grandparents. "Moster" Signe was

always cheerful and gay, and the atmosphere of contented spontaneity in Kalundborg was doubtless due to her influence. In Trondheim, she later recalled, there were masses of water lilies which grew in such luxuriant abundance, "broad bright streets where the sun and the breeze from the fjord had such power," and "the strange red evening light which you saw there and nowhere else in the world." [5]

Her parents had only a small circle of friends, for the most part colleagues of her father, with whom they shared common interests. They were "Liberals" who discussed the question of Norway's full equality within the Swedish-dominated dual monarchy. The young girl may not have been interested in such political talk, but she listened with attentive ear when the conversation turned to such topics as the Lion Gate of Mycenae, the ruins of Tiryns, the story of Agamemnon and Clytemnestra, or the siege of Troy. As a child she played with a small terracotta horse from Troy which the famous Heinrich Schliemann had given her father. Ingvald Undset may have cherished dreams that his oldest daughter might follow in his footsteps as a scholar, but he could hardly have suspected that she was to gain fame in richer measure as one of Norway's most gifted writers.

After some early instruction at home from her father and mother Sigrid Undset was sent to the private coeducational school of the liberally oriented Fru Ragna Nielsen. Although she was a better-than-average pupil, Sigrid Undset was never interested in any formal education, but preferred to use her own reason in arriving at any basic truth. From her father she had already learned much more than she now read in the textbooks. When in school many views which she considered untenable were presented as facts, she came to believe that every statement must be taken with a grain of salt. One must learn to use one's own mind, the children were told, "but if one really took the trouble to think for oneself and arrived at conclusions different from those expected by the teachers, one was nevertheless supposed to think as they wished." [6]

Despite her mother's objection to all sentimental and sensational juvenile literature Sigrid Undset nevertheless managed to read her share of dime novels and Indian stories. In the maid's room, to which she had access, she read surreptitiously cheap romances bearing such titles as *A Falling Star on Ekeberg* or *The*

Bergen Regicide, or the Bloody Wedding at Nidaros. However, she was not blind to their poor literary quality and there was something in these romances which reminded her "of tainted water that had been forgotten in a carafe, or of all the foul and unwholesome smells whereby the town became familiar to her senses." [7] The translations of sentimental German stories which were read in school she considered strange and quite insipid and she found the girls in Louisa May Alcott's *Little Women* so sweet that they were insufferable.[8] There was a definite charm, however, in the humor of Ludvig Holberg, even though she did not understand everything in *Niels Klim's Journey Underground* or *Peder Paars,* which she knew almost by heart. It was all so splendidly exciting, and the many funny drawings became dear to her. Elling Holst's *Norse Picture Book for Children,* the fairy tales of Hans Christian Andersen, and the folk tales collected by Jörgen Moe and Peter Christen Asbjörnsen, were also part of the living tradition of Sigrid Undset's youth and among the books that exerted the greatest influence upon her in her childhood.[9]

However, she enjoyed more serious reading too. Soon after she had learned her ABC's she was given Siegwart Petersen's *History of Norway* to read. She had to spell her way through a certain section each day and on the following day repeat the substance of what she had read before going on to the next section. Sigrid Undset's mother, as a gesture of patriotic pride, also had her read N. C. Rom's *History of Denmark.* The young girl preferred this book because it was a straightforward little text designed for elementary schools.[10]

One day she was glancing at the illustrations in her father's six-volume set of Daae and Drolsum's *History of the World.* Jokingly her father challenged her to read through all six volumes for two crowns. It took the young girl two years to plough her way through the ponderous work, and later she was surprised to find out how little she remembered of it.[11] Nevertheless, she liked whatever she read. She was never terrified of the printed page, even if she understood nothing. It merely gave her something to puzzle over, and when she read the books over and over again, she found that she could digest a little more each time.

In her formative years she could not look upon the study of history in the same light as her father, who was trained in the scholarly disciplines necessary for proper historical interpretation.

However, through association with him she must have acquired some feeling for the distinction between historical fact and fancy which she was later to reveal in her medieval novels.

As a child Sigrid Undset was given only a conventional religious upbringing. The religious skepticism of her parents was typical of many progressive homes at the turn of the century. To be sure, she and her sisters were taught to say their evening prayers, and on Christmas Eve her mother read the Christmas gospel and sang hymns from her Danish hymn book. Anna Charlotte Undset preferred to believe that God was distant and did not interfere in the lives of men. However, "if God opposed the proud and gave His grace to the humble, then she wouldn't have anything to do with Him. She was not humble—and Seming [name for Sigrid Undset's father in *The Longest Years*] had no reason to be humble, but enough and more than enough to be proud of." [12] Her mother's defiance frightened Sigrid. At the same time it seemed to her that it was madness for anyone to venture to say what God ought to be, once he believed that God did not interfere in the lives of men.

Her father's God was an "invisible spirit which men felt within and around them, and to the end of the world men would never be able to express clearly what it was of God that they felt." [13] As a boy Ingvald Undset had been distrustful of the many Protestant sects and religiously minded circles in small towns and in the country. He was especially annoyed with the ministers and lay "leaders" who flocked among them. "The Catholics were satisfied to have *one* pope, said Seming, and he was only infallible when he spoke *ex cathedra,* but the Christian communities of friends here in the North cheerfully put up with popes by the dozen, and they were infallible whether they spoke in the meeting house or over a richly laden dinner table, *ex* the pulpit or *ex* their galoshes." [14] Ingvald Undset had come far from the rock-bound faith of his father in Trondheim, who always spoke of God's will and the good gifts He bestows upon all who have sufficient understanding to accept all with the gratitude of faith in Jesus' name.[15]

Sigrid Undset did not know what she should believe. To her, God was an invisible and omniscient spirit beyond the circle of night and day, but she did not necessarily think it reassuring to know that He was constantly at hand and concerned with her. For the time being she wished merely to be free of all care. She could agree neither with those people who with Grundtvigian optimism looked upon Christianity as something mild and comfortable nor with those who spoke of God as an irascible and vindictive magistrate of whom one had to beware continually.

When she was being prepared for confirmation by an orthodox Lutheran West End clergyman, she was given his version of the orthodox Lutheran God of upper-class Christiania. Then she realized that everyone imagined God just as he would prefer Him to be. She too had her own ideas of God, but she was reasonable enough to concede that her ideas were not necessarily acceptable to anyone else. She was confused and had no positive belief in anything.

After her father's death in December, 1893, Sigrid Undset was given the opportunity to continue at the progressive school of Ragna Nielsen without payment of tuition until matriculation at the university. However, she had no desire to study further at school, for even as a thirteen-year-old girl she had become disillusioned with the "liberal" ideas of Ragna Nielsen and the sentimental enthusiasm of her teachers and was beginning to believe that the liberals were the most bigoted of all people. Furthermore, the thought of university life had never occurred to her as a possibility. At that time she was much more interested in becoming a painter. At Dröbak in the summer of 1894 she met Theodor Kittelsen, who was well known for his pictures from the Lofoten Islands and his illustrations of Norwegian folk tales. He recognized the young girl's talent, but discouraged her from studying painting. He explained that a painter cannot derive any pleasure from his art, for he is never satisfied with what he has accomplished, but always dreams of producing something better. On a journey which leads to no goal he experiences nothing but humiliation, poverty, and intrigue. Talent may be a gift, but it is also a curse.[16]

II Office Employment (1899–1909). Early Writings

With the intention of becoming self-supporting as soon as possible Sigrid Undset at the age of fifteen passed her middle-school examination and then enrolled at the Christiania Commercial College. After receiving a certificate from this school a year later, she accepted a position in the local office of the German Electric Company. Although office work was not to her liking, she held this position for ten years and proved to be a most efficient typist and secretary.

The office experience of these years was in many ways of inestimable value to the young girl. Although she had lived all her life in Christiania and was familiar with every nook and cranny of the town, she had nevertheless until now felt rootless in the big city. At last she began to make the town her home. She had the time and opportunity to wander farther afield through the outlying districts and found the city and its surroundings just as beautiful in one season as in another.

She now came into contact with people quite different from the academic friends of her parents. There were the engineers, secretaries, and clerks in offices, shop girls and store keepers in town, and young people in cafés, boarding houses, and rented rooms. She observed them carefully, so that she might better understand their thinking and their actions, and thus made them all part of her own consciousness. In 1910 she said in an interview: "For me, Oslo is the most beautiful town in the world, its people the most delightful, their speech, in its every nuance from Homansby to Ekeberg, the most joyous means of expression for human thought." [17]

Her summer holidays were spent either with relatives in Kalundborg and Trondheim or in the mountains above Gudbrandsdal. She felt especially drawn to the mountains, and hardly anywhere in Norwegian literature has their magnificent grandeur been described with greater love and feeling than in her works.

During these years of office employment Sigrid Undset made wise use of every spare moment to increase her knowledge of both Norwegian and foreign literature and history. Mrs. Ragnhild Undset Wiberg, one of the author's two younger sisters, writes that Sigrid considered nothing less than eighteen hours to be a normal working day.[18] Inspired by Georg Brandes' book on Shakespeare, she proceeded to read not only the works of the great dramatist, but also as much as possible of Elizabethan literature. In addition she read, among many others, the works of Dickens, Fielding, Burns, Sir Thomas More, and especially the lyric poetry of Shelley and Keats. She also became better acquainted with the works of Norwegian writers from Ibsen and Björnson to Nils Collett Vogt, Jonas Lie, Gunnar Heiberg, and Amalie Skram. Above

all she was drawn to the Middle Ages, to which she had first been
introduced by her father. She was fascinated by the medieval ballads, the German minnesingers, folk songs, sagas, legends, and
indeed anything pertaining to history. Once, when only eighteen,
she borrowed from the library Unger's edition of *Heilagra manna
sögur*, a collection of stories and legends of holy men and women.
The librarian observed that the book had not been out on loan
since it was published in 1877! [19]

With such extensive reading, particularly of literary and historical material of the Middle Ages, Sigrid Undset was preparing the
foundation for her creative writing. In 1902 she wrote to a Swedish friend that she was working on a historical novel which had its
setting in Norway in the middle of the thirteenth century. A few
years later the novel was finished and submitted in person to the
Gyldendal publishing house in Copenhagen. Upon her second
visit to Copenhagen the manuscript was returned to her by Peter
Nansen, the director of Gyldendal, with the friendly advice that
she turn her hand to something modern which would be more
suited to her talents. Sigrid Undset followed Nansen's advice and
began work on *Fru Marta Oulie* (*Mrs. Marta Oulie*), a novel
written in diary form and beginning with Marta Oulie's confession: "I have been unfaithful to my husband." Surely this was
modern enough!

This time the manuscript was submitted to H. Aschehoug & Co.
in Oslo. At first it was again rejected, but later with the help of an
enthusiastic endorsement by Gunnar Heiberg, one of the leading
dramatists of the time, *Mrs. Marta Oulie* was accepted by this
publisher, and the novel appeared in the fall of 1907. Its theme of
infidelity in marriage is quite common in modern Norwegian literature and one which Sigrid Undset used again in 1908 in a one-act
play *I graalysningen* (*In the Gray Light of Dawn*). The characters described in these two early works are drawn from the middle-
class world in which she had been raised and which she knew so
well. They are commonplace people who live out their lives in the
drab atmosphere of the capital city at the turn of the century.

In 1908 Sigrid Undset also published a collection of short stories
ironically entitled *Den lykkelige alder* (*The Happy Age*), in
which she draws a vivid picture of young Oslo working girls like
herself who live with their hopes and dreams of happiness. These

girls find their work uninteresting and the conditions of life which surround them dull and monotonous, but they are made of sturdy moral fiber and despite their loneliness of heart they continue in their search for something or someone worthy of their complete faith and devotion.

The same note of melancholy longing is also to be found in some of Sigrid Undset's poems. She wrote three of them for the journal *Samtiden* in 1908, and others were published in a collection entitled *Ungdom (Youth)* in 1910. These poems represent her sole attempt at verse, and although they are not good poetry, they reveal that the former agnostic is expressing her longing for some divinity which she might worship.

After these two stories of modern life Sigrid Undset, disregarding the advice of Peter Nansen, returned in 1909 to the field of historical fiction with the publication of *Fortellingen om Viga-Ljot og Vigdis* (tr. as *Gunnar's Daughter*), a saga-pastiche which has its setting in tenth-century Norway and Iceland. In *The Longest Years* she tells of her introduction to the Icelandic sagas by her father and the thrill with which she first read *Njál's Saga.*[20] During her father's long illness she used to read to him selections from the sagas, usually in translation, but at times in the original, although she could probably understand only very little of the Old Icelandic text. In *Gunnar's Daughter* the writer reveals considerable historical perspective, although there are many stylistic features of a descriptive and dramatic nature which are not characteristic of the saga.

III Rome and Oslo (1909–1912)

After the publication of three moderately successful works Sigrid Undset felt sufficient confidence in her writing ability to give up her secretarial position. In 1909 she received a travel grant of 3,000 crowns from the Norwegian government and went to Rome where she stayed until the summer of 1910. There she met her future husband, the artist Anders C. Svarstad. The letters she wrote from here to the newspaper *Aftenposten* in Oslo give an indication of the joyous feeling which the young writer experienced in her new environment. Rome and the beautiful Campagna offered her a welcome release from the monotony and routine of office employment. She spent many pleasant evenings in the company of a small group of friends who listened with rapt attention to her retelling of stories and legends from the Middle Ages.

She often visited churches, and although impressed by the esthetic beauty of the Catholic service, she had as yet no interest in or understanding of its spiritual message. Indeed, in a letter written from Rome at Whitsuntide, 1910, she revealed her complete indifference to the celebration of this particular holy day.[21]

From Rome Sigrid Undset went to Paris and then returned to Oslo in the fall. At this time she became acquainted with the writer Nini Roll Anker, with whom she shared a common interest in the much discussed issue of women's rights. In her little book about Sigrid Undset (*Min venn Sigrid Undset*, 1946) Mrs. Anker has given an informative account of their friendship during the following years.[22] Other frequent visitors at the Undset home were the lyric poet Nils Collett Vogt and the novelists Kristian Elster, Jr., and Peter Egge.

In 1911 Sigrid Undset published her first full-length novel, *Jenny*, the tragic love story of a young woman artist who commits suicide when she finds that she cannot live up to the high moral standards she has set for herself. Although she has achieved moderate success as an artist, Jenny is convinced that the ultimate destiny of any woman is not her work, which is self-gratifying and therefore basically selfish, but complete identification with some man whom she can love and respect. She has faith in her own strength, and believes that it will be she who has failed if she does not find this happiness.

On two occasions she drifts into love affairs which prove to be degrading and humiliating. In moments of weakness and on the basis of physical gratification alone she allows herself to make commitments when her deeper feelings are not involved. In accepting love when she has nothing to offer in return, she betrays her better self. Jenny is torn between her own erotic tendencies and her inability to prove adequate to the men who love her. She becomes discouraged and despondent because she feels that she has thrown away a precious part of herself. It follows almost of necessity that Jenny takes her own life, because with her severe moral idealism she cannot adjust to any superficial standard of values which would take such casual affairs lightly.

Jenny was Sigrid Undset's most successful novel to date and it was also the first to be translated into English. It was, however, a controversial novel and the topic for discussion at many women's club meetings. Nini Roll Anker writes of one such discussion held in the Grand Hotel in Oslo on February 19, 1912, with about 300 women in attendance, including the writers Barbra Ring, Fernanda Nissen, and Regine Normann. Mrs. Anker reports that the meeting came close to breaking up in disorder, while Sigrid Undset was the only one who remained calm and unperturbed. She did not take part in the discussion, but when she was asked whether she was offended and disappointed, she merely answered: "No, on the contrary, I didn't expect anything else." [23]

The reading public was aroused at the frank and realistic description of erotic experience and details of pregnancy and childbirth in the novel. Militant feminists also believed that the image of the emancipated woman was damaged by Jenny who runs away from life when she is no longer able to find fulfillment in her work. Mrs. Anker adds that *Jenny* thus underwent a baptism of fire, but after the success of the novel all had to concede that Norway now had a woman writer whose name was to be reckoned among the greatest.[24]

IV *London and Rome (1912–1913). Oslo (1913–1919)*

In the spring of 1912 Sigrid Undset was married to the artist Anders Castus Svarstad in a civil ceremony in Antwerp. Svarstad, thirteen years her senior, was a divorced man with three children by his former marriage. He was an artist of considerable talent and best known through his paintings of scenes from the industrial section of Oslo such as *Factory Girl* (1902) and *Myren's Workshop in Oslo* (1903).

From Antwerp the couple went to London where they lived in Hammersmith. From letters written to Mrs. Anker, it is evident that this was the most carefree time Sigrid Undset was to enjoy for many years to come. While her husband painted (*Factory on the Thames*, 1912), she read English literature of the Renaissance period and worked on a collection of short stories to which she gave the title *Fattige skjebner (Poor Fortunes*, 1912). In these stories she writes of unfortunate ordinary people living in Oslo at the turn of the century. They are described with humor and a mild irony, but with a warm understanding for the weaknesses in all human nature. She surrounds the destinies of these poor drudges with a certain glow which reflects her growing spiritual consciousness and her literary skill.

In December, 1912, Sigrid Undset and her husband returned to Rome where they had met during her first visit there in 1909. At that time Svarstad had painted a portrait of Sigrid Undset, which is now in the Rasmus Meyer Collections in Bergen. Her first child, Anders, was born in January, 1913. When the infant's health did not progress satisfactorily, she returned to Oslo and for several months stayed with her mother. In July she rented two rooms at Ski, close enough to Oslo so that Svarstad could have a studio in the city.

In March, 1914, Sigrid Undset delivered an address in the Students' Union in Oslo on the topic "The Fourth Commandment." She spoke not only of the obligation of children to honor their parents, but also of the obligation which parents have to conduct their lives in such a way that their children *can* honor them. High moral concepts must be taught early in life, so that the cultured individual may be aware not only of his rights, but also of his duties and obligations, for the higher the culture the greater the responsibility. Civilized man has achieved great technical and cultural progress, but in order that this cultural heritage may be preserved, he must also have a sense of reverence and obedience. Because religion and culture are so closely related, civilized man has created after his own image a God who is a symbol, though not the source, of all good.

Despite all household and family responsibilities she continued to write, and in the autumn of 1914 she published another long novel *Vaaren* (*Spring*). Stylistically, *Spring* has its weaknesses, with too many flashbacks, particularly at the beginning, and numerous passages which seem irrelevant to the main action. However, the novel presents a very sensitive treatment of the love and marriage of a young couple, who must undergo many trials before they can establish a complete harmony and integrity in their relationship. Rose and Torkild are noble-minded young people, unwilling to accept the self-seeking marital views of the time. They find happiness in their marriage only because they make serious demands of themselves and remain loyal to the principles to which they are committed.

In 1915, soon after the outbreak of war, Sigrid Undset pub-

lished her *Fortellinger om Kong Artur og ridderne av det runde
bord* (*Tales of King Arthur and the Knights of the Round Table*).
In this work, which has strong religious overtones, she pays a stirring tribute to the indomitable spirit of the English people.

A second child, Maren Charlotte, was born in October, 1915,
and at times Sigrid Undset also had her three stepchildren living
with her. Mrs. Anker, a frequent visitor at Ski, has given a very
striking description of Sigrid Undset at this time. She writes:
"Whenever she presided over the white tablecloth, in the paneled
living room, sitting up straight with her hair plaited over the back
of her head in big bright braids, her movements quiet and calm as
she dispensed food and drink to us guests, there was always a
gentle dignity about her which reminded me of the household
mistresses of times long past." [25]

In the summer of 1916 Sigrid Undset moved to the East Aker
section of Oslo. Mrs. Anker writes that the next three years must
have been the most difficult period in Sigrid Undset's life. Her
three stepchildren came to live with her again, and the entire care
of children and household lay in her hands. It now became evident that her young daughter Maren, or "Tulla" as she was affec-
tionately called, was a mentally retarded child who required her
mother's constant attention. At no time, however, did Sigrid Undset entertain the thought of placing the child in an institution.
Until she died at the age of twenty-three, Maren was kept at
home and given all the loving care and devotion of a gravely concerned mother.

With great determination and will power Sigrid Undset continued to write and in 1917 she published *Splinten av troldspeilet*
(*Images in a Mirror*) and in 1918 *De kloge jomfruer* (*The Wise
Virgins*). In the original Norwegian the former volume consists of
two short stories, *Fru Hjelde* (*Mrs. Hjelde*) and *Fru Waage*
(*Mrs. Waage*), both of which are concerned with young women
who are faced with the harsh realities confronting them in married life. The literal translation of the Norwegian title is *The
Splinter of the Troll Mirror* with an obvious reference to the
magic mirror which, according to Hans Christian Andersen,
makes people see things in distortion. In contrast to Harriet
Waage, Uni Hjelde is able to remove the splinter or mote from
her eye and view her marriage in a more realistic light. In return

for romantic illusion she has found true happiness in the love and
devotion which as a married woman she can offer husband and
children within the framework of the family circle.

Like *Poor Fortunes, The Wise Virgins* deals with characters
from the working class of Oslo, and the basic theme is again that
of maternal love. Sigrid Undset shows great compassion for the
self-sacrificing middle-aged spinsters who have not known this
deepest of human emotions. In these stories she seems to make an
implicit plea for poor unfortunate women who are often subjected
to ridicule and abuse. She affirms that all are part of common
humanity and as human beings have the right to exist with dignity
and respect.

From 1912 to 1919 Sigrid Undset wrote a series of articles deal-
ing with the question of women's rights and the role of the mother
in contemporary society. These articles express views similar to
those clearly implied in her fiction and were published in a single
volume in 1919 under the title *Et kvindesynspunkt* (*A Woman's
Point of View*).[26]

As an emancipated woman herself she had great sympathy and
understanding for those women who in their fight for political and
economic rights had to suffer ridicule, but she was opposed to any
newly acquired freedom which was construed as a "privilege"
rather than as an "obligation." For her the question of equality
between the sexes did not arise. Of chief importance in human
society was woman's natural desire for home and children. If the
emancipated woman could not harmonize her newly-won rights
with her role as a mother, she could nevertheless still find happiness simply in being a mother, for she considered motherhood,
with all its duties and obligations, but also its little joys, to be the
real reason for living. She writes: "Any woman who becomes a
good mother is greater than most ministers of state, for she is in-
dispensable in her work, whereas very many ministers can be replaced with advantage." [27]

During these same years 1912–1919 one may observe a very
definite development in Sigrid Undset's religious thinking. As a
child she had heard very little talk of religion at home, and yet in
spite of this she had followed her natural impulses in believing
that the Divine was something transcendent with which she had a
certain, though indefinite, relationship. While being prepared for
confirmation, however, she began to understand that everyone be-

lieved God to be as he or she wished Him to be. Seeking a more positive objective truth she could not accept everyone else's personal representation of God.

In a letter which she wrote to Mrs. Anker in 1915 she comments: "Mama frets a little now and then because she did not manage to teach us religion. There is nothing for which I am more grateful to her than for the healthy un-Christian atmosphere in our home." [28] She adds:

"I have never had any ill-will toward Christianity, simply because I scarcely knew what it was. I viewed the Church as an extremely picturesque ruin standing in the background of the landscape. In later years I looked at it a little more closely. I have learned a little from what the priests write, etc. I have also read a number of Catholic authors, both new and old. The Church of Rome has form at any rate; it does not have an irritating effect on one's intelligence as do these diverse 'Protestant' sects. If one takes away the form given to it by the Church of Rome, all Christianity has the effect on me of an unsuccessful broken omelet." [29]

In her lecture on the Fourth Commandment (1914) Sigrid Undset refers to the close relationship between culture and religion. She acknowledges the concept of God merely as a symbol created by man. Five years later, however, in "Efterskrift" ("Postscript," 1919), God is no longer conceived as an idea but as a concrete reality and Christianity as a historical fact which teaches that man is created in God's image.

Professor Winsnes has pointed out that Sigrid Undset experienced no *choc spirituel* which made her suddenly see the world in a completely new light. It was a gradual process during which Christianity was revealed to her as a confirmation of what thought and experience had already taught her. Her intellectual honesty would have made it impossible for her to reject Christianity before she knew what Christianity was.[30]

V *Lillehammer (1919–1940)*

In July, 1919, Sigrid Undset moved to Lillehammer on Lake Mjösa at the southern entrance to the Gudbrandsdal valley. The following month she gave birth to her third child, Hans. For the first fifteen months at Lillehammer she rented a house, but then she purchased an old house which had been moved from a farm in

Sör-Fron to Lillehammer by its previous owner. In 1924 she bought a second old house which was floated down the Laagen River from Sel in Gudbrandsdal. She called her new home "Bjerkebæk" to irritate her Danish relatives, as she said.[31] Svarstad visited the family occasionally at Lillehammer, but the rift between husband and wife continued to grow and the marriage was finally annulled when Sigrid Undset was received into the Catholic Church on All Saints' Day, November 24, 1924.

Lillehammer was to be Sigrid Undset's home for the next twenty years, years which proved to be the happiest and most productive of her whole life. She experienced great pride and joy in furnishing her new home in such a way as to combine distinctive features of her own age with those of times long past. Rooms and window sills overflowed with an abundance of flowers and plants. At one time she had about four hundred varieties of plants growing in her home and garden.[32]

Fundamentally she was happy in simply being a loving and devoted mother to her children. This happiness is probably best reflected in the charming account of life in Norway as described in *Lykkelige dager* (*Happy Days in Norway*, 1942), a children's book written while she was living in exile in the United States (1940–1945). The reader follows the life of a single family through the cycle of one year. The family described is her own at Lillehammer, and the time is the period before the Nazi occupation of her homeland. One shares in all the joys of holidays and festive occasions as they are celebrated within the intimate family circle. Sigrid Undset writes of vacations in the mountains and life on a *sæter* (mountain farm), of history and folk tales, of traditions and customs. *Happy Days in Norway* is somewhat of an anomaly among Sigrid Undset's works, for here the usually somber world of darker coloration has been transformed into one filled with sunshine and laughter. In this work as in no other, the author has revealed her abiding love for the natural beauties of her native land and the deep affection which she felt for all children.

At Lillehammer she again returned to her historical studies. In 1905 Peter Nansen had advised the young author to concern herself henceforth with material from contemporary life. With the exception of *Gunnar's Daughter* (1909), written in imitation of the Old Icelandic sagas, and *Tales of King Arthur and the Knights of the Round Table* (1915) she had followed this advice for fifteen years, but from 1920 to 1927 she wrote the two great medieval novels which were to win her international literary fame: *Kristin Lavransdatter* and *Olav Audunssön*. Almost immediately both novels became best-sellers in Germany and the United States as well as in Norway. In 1928 she was awarded the Nobel Prize for Literature, the third Norwegian, with Björnson (1903) and Hamsun (1920), to be so honored.

Kristin Lavransdatter appeared in three parts. The first of these, *Kransen* (*The Bridal Wreath*), was published in 1920, the second, *Husfrue* (*The Mistress of Husaby*), in 1921, and the third, *Korset* (*The Cross*), in 1922. Three years later the first part of her second historical novel, *Olav Audunssön i Hestviken* (*Olav Audunssön of Hestviken*), appeared, and the second part, *Olav Audunssön og hans börn* (*Olav Audunssön and His Children*), appeared in 1927.

Both novels were written while she was under unceasing pressure of household duties. Only after the children were in bed would she sit at her desk and with cigarettes and black coffee as stimulants write until two or three o'clock in the morning. During the day there were newspapers and books, old laws, and all kinds of old documents to be read. Her first concern, however, was always the happiness and well-being of her children. Hers was a happy home in which her friends always found a warm welcome.

Although she was disillusioned with the materialism and the neo-paganism of her own age, her interest in the Middle Ages was by no means an escape into a romantic dreamworld. At the beginning of the twentieth century scholars had long since given up the belief that the Middle Ages represented a spiritual vacuum between the brilliant culture of classical antiquity and the period of enlightenment in the eighteenth century. They now saw in the Middle Ages a great creative period in which, through the organization and spread of Christianity, new advances were made in the culture and civilization of the European community.

Not all scholars, however, were willing to concede that Scandinavia, even after its conversion to Christianity, had been part of this "universal" European civilization. In his short story *Mot ballade*, for example, the writer Hans E. Kinck maintained that the heroic spirit of the North was best typified in the classical Icelandic saga and that contact with Christianity had merely hindered the free development of the spiritual life of this pagan society. The historian Edvard Bull believed that it would have been

impossible for the Church to teach sturdy Norwegian farmers of
the eleventh, twelfth, and thirteenth centuries to accept the Christian doctrine of humility, much less that of sin and grace.[33]

Fredrik Paasche, on the other hand, one of the greatest authori-
ties on the Middle Ages, was able to present very telling evidence
that Christianity had indeed been a living force in the religious
life of the Norwegian people. He called attention to the large
quantity of Old Norse Christian literature, for the most part translated from Latin, which had been overlooked by scholars. Collections of sermons, such as the Old Norwegian book of homilies
entitled *Homilíubók,* and of stories and legends of holy men and
saints, such as *Heilagra manna sögur,* reveal quite clearly that it
was contact with Europe and the acquisition of Christian civilization that made the greatest impact on the culture of medieval
Norway.[34]

Sigrid Undset, too, was engaged in independent research. In an
excellent essay on the old ballads, entitled "Om folkeviser" and
written in 1921, she points out the close relationship between the
popular didactic literature and the religious element of the ballad.[35]

Her keen interest in the Middle Ages is also shown in her translations of three Old Icelandic sagas published in 1923,[36] as well as
in the narrative *Sankt Halvards liv, död og jertegn* (*Saint Halvard's Life, Death, and Miracles,* 1925),[37] the historical narrative
Hellig Olav, Norges konge (*Saint Olav, King of Norway,* 1930),[38]
in which she gives a popular account of the introduction of Christianity in Norway, and in three scholarly essays which she prepared for J. W. Cappelen's *Norwegian Cultural History.*[39]

Sigrid Undset's interest in historical studies was awakened early
in life by her father and the scholarly atmosphere in her home.
She felt that she had been brought up in a pervading historical
ambience in which all sharp distinctions between past and present
were merged. In 1919 she wrote to her friend Mrs. Anker: "I think
the reason why I understand our own time so well, or see it so
clearly, is because ever since I was a child I have had some kind
of living memory from an earlier age to compare with it." [40] But if
the past taught her something of the present, so too did the present throw much light on the past, for she believed that the human
heart has not changed in the least down through the ages in spite
of differences in manners and customs. Men and women were

stirred by the same emotions then as they are today. She was interested primarily in the eternal conflicts of the heart and soul. The historical background, accurately though it has been portrayed, is merely an incidental accessory. In reference to her historical novels, Victor Vinde has written: "She wished to portray the emotional world of a fifteenth century individual, without regard to anecdote or historical fact. Thus she has not written an 'historical novel,' but a novel in which men of the Middle Ages live. It is their thoughts and their reactions which interest us—in short, their inner lives." [41]

It is difficult to trace the last steps in Sigrid Undset's discovery of Christianity. In her account of how she became a Catholic and why she remained in the Church ("Hvordan jeg blev katolikk og hvorfor jeg er det i dag"), she writes that she had always believed in the existence of one single truth. Because everything is already arranged by law, one must find his way to this truth through a chain of cause and effect. However, she adds: "It was a long time before I had the courage to conceive of a God who was the 'Absolute Other,' yet at the same time a Person who could hold communion with me—whose ways were not my ways, whose will could be separated unconditionally and definitely from my will, but who could, nevertheless, lead me into His ways and bring my will into harmony with His own." [42]

She turned to the Catholic Church as the sole authority, because the inner logic of its teachings appealed to her intellect. The Reformation in her opinion was nothing other than a revolt against Christianity. By its very opposition to Catholicism Protestantism could not be the true bearer of the Christian tradition because it had lost direct historical continuity with the old Church.

The Catholic belief in the doctrine of one legitimate authority was also important for her. The Catholic Church was not an "organization," but an "organism" in which man is not an independent individual, but a living cell in a body. He may also be likened to a branch which withers and dies if it is cut off from the tree. For the many Protestant sects and congregations in Norway, on the other hand, authority in matters of faith was simply a matter of subjective experience.

Sigrid Undset also saw in Catholicism an open attitude toward the realities of life and the free development of individual person-

ality. She was opposed to any puritanical morality which preferred to ignore the sexual instinct as a positive factor in human
experience. With her strong sensuality she believed that an attitude of "pretend not to see" was responsible for the hypocrisy and
moral anarchy of her time. Erotic passion releases mighty forces
which elevate man to the greatest heights, but physical love has
no rights of its own when it comes into conflict with moral and
ethical laws. This is a thought which finds a constant echo in her
entire literary production.

Like many other converts, Sigrid Undset must have been impressed with the beauty of the Catholic church and its service.
One has only to recall the beautiful scene in which she describes
Kristin Lavransdatter's first visit to the cathedral at Hamar.[43] The
mighty Gothic structure appears to the heroine as a revelation of
God's power and glory, and in the play of the sunlight filtering
through the stained glass windows she beholds a vision of daz-
zling beauty.

The description of the Nidaros Cathedral in the evening sun,
when Kristin makes her first pilgrimage to the shrine of St. Olav,
is just as overpowering. This time she sees the beauty of the richly
sculptured cathedral in relation to her own sinful self.[44] Here as
elsewhere we find a sublime expression of the Catholic's love for
the church as the house of the living God. For Sigrid Undset the
beauty of light and color has its rightful place in the worship of
God just as in nature itself. No segment of life is to be disregarded, but is to be viewed in relationship to the divine.

At the same time it is also true that in her polemic against Protestantism Sigrid Undset lacks the objective judgment which one
might expect of a woman of great intellect. Carl F. Engelstad
writes that one often gains the impression that she identifies Protestantism with some of its negative manifestations and out-
growths and closes her eyes to what is genuine in it. According to
her own statement she came to Catholicism "from the outside"
and was not familiar with Protestantism "from the inside." [45] In
any case, Sigrid Undset had come to accept Christianity as the
one objective reality, and in the Catholic Church she had found to
her own satisfaction the manifestation of this reality.

She spent the Easter holidays of 1925 in Italy with her mother
and son Anders. In a letter published in the Christmas annual *Det
kimer i klokker* she describes the church service at Monte Cas-

sino and thus throws some light on her own religious experience. She writes:

All these tens of thousands in the church, believers and doubters and unbelievers, the prayerful and the curious, good Catholics and bad Catholics—the first pope in his tomb and all the popes who are at rest around him, and the last pope who kneels in prayer, while around him now prayers rise up from this church like the flood-tide. The prayers spread themselves like an atmosphere among those who pray and those who do not pray, as does the cry that mounts up to all those who have gone before, innumerable myriads of dead Christians, begging that they too will pray with us. I cannot explain it properly: it is, I feel, as if the names of ideas which I have accepted purely with my intellect were suddenly illuminated by an object-lesson. The Christian congregation, the catholicity of the Church, the communion of the saints, the relative reality of time and space and, outside the eggshell, the absolute reality of eternity, the untold souls who have lived through the ages, each of them imprisoned in the ravelled net of his own self, from which no doctrine can set us free, only God, and He only by dying on a cross. One can recognise it as the only thing which makes sense in the end: one can understand it, but sometimes it seems as if one can *see* it. . . . Something of the kind I can see this evening also—the fleetingness of time and every event, the reality of eternity and of the spirit; but actually I see it bare of ceremony, as a sober truth—even so, it is no less overwhelming.[46]

In two articles written in 1927 Sigrid Undset attacks Luther, the secularization of the Lutheran Church, and its submission to the State. These articles are entitled "Hvad katolisismen mener om Luther" ("What Catholicism Thinks of Luther"), which appeared in the Catholic journal *St. Olav*, and "Lutherdommens aand og katolisismen" ("The Lutheran Spirit and Catholicism"), published in the newspaper *Aftenposten*. In a third article, "Katolsk propaganda" ("Catholic Propaganda"), which first appeared in Ronald Fangen's conservative periodical *Vor Verden* in 1927, she takes issue with the Lutheran doctrine of salvation by faith alone and the bondage of the human will. Here she speaks of God as the one legitimate authority, the *auctor vitae*. In addition to his ordered life on earth man has also an eternal destiny. As a good Catholic, Sigrid Undset believed that the human will, far from being enslaved, was free to choose between good and evil. She writes: "No human being shall be saved unless he wills it so himself, and none condemned unless it is his will, choosing this rather than allowing his will to harmonize with the will of God." [47] Elsewhere she expresses this same thought more bluntly by using the image taken from a medieval sermon: "You can lead a horse to water, but you can't make him drink." [48]

After the completion of her two medieval novels Sigrid Undset returned to contemporary themes with the publication of *Gymnadenia* (*The Wild Orchid*) in 1929 and its sequel *Den brennende busk* (*The Burning Bush*) in 1930. These two novels tell the story of Paul Selmer's conversion to Catholicism, and at first glance might be considered as a reflection of the author's own religious experience. In a sense all of her works have something of an autobiographical nature, although the external circumstances which surround the characters of her novels have no similarity to the facts of her own life. There is, however, a similarity on the spiritual plane, for Paul Selmer and Sigrid Undset do have the same intellectual qualities; both are of a skeptical temperament, and their logically thinking minds are completely unsatisfied with the prejudices of the bourgeois liberalism and sentimental humanitarianism of the early part of the century. In his search for an objective truth, Paul Selmer rejects the primacy of worldly success or enlightened self-interest or any other of the modern substitute religions. He has an instinctive feeling that this objective truth is to be found in a Christian spiritual world which transcends the everyday world created by man after his own image in his selfish and arbitrary manner. He is drawn to the Church because its laws correspond to the needs of his own moral nature. Here he finds a metaphysical foundation for his faith, for, according to the dogma of the Church, God is the one eternal truth. He has created man and given him a supernatural destiny to work His will on earth and through His grace to be prepared for eternity.

In her next two novels, *Ida Elisabeth* (1932) and *Den trofaste hustru* (*The Faithful Wife*, 1933), the religious idea is again present, although it does not manifest itself with the same directness as in *The Wild Orchid* and *The Burning Bush*. Both novels are realistic studies of women who react with all intelligence to problems which arise out of their marriages. Sigrid Undset examines the sacramental nature of marriage, through which both parties are bound in an indissoluble union, not primarily to further their own welfare on earth, but to accept the duties and responsibilities

to God and to each other in God. She felt that marriage as a sacrament rather than as a contract was instituted to help people on
the road to salvation, for she was realistic enough to know that
men and women have never been faithful unless their fidelity
transcends mere human relationships.

She strips sexual love of all romantic illusions and considers
only the responsibilities involved in the marital relationship. Because marriage has been raised to a spiritual plane by being a
sacrament, husband and wife must consider themselves bound
even in an unhappy marriage. In an essay "Brev til en sogneprest"
("Reply to a Parish Priest," 1930), she writes: "If the delinquen-
cies of one party are of such a nature as to render cohabitation
impossible, the other must nevertheless feel himself bound to such
an extent that he or she works for the welfare of both their souls,
by prayer and penance and good deeds." [49]

In Ida Elisabeth and Nathalie (*The Faithful Wife*) Sigrid Undset has drawn portraits of two noble-minded and loyal women
who seek stable values in a time of crisis. There is deep human
significance in the manner in which they accept their responsibilities. Because they act according to their own natures rather than
from any religious scruples, their high moral qualities are all the
more persuasive. These women are alive and real, and the choices
they make are implicit in the characters themselves.

In her contemporary novels as well as in a series of essays written after the completion of *Kristin Lavransdatter* and *Olav
Audunssön*, Sigrid Undset is quite critical of the materialistic
trend in modern civilization. It is clear to her that "enlightened"
idealism, sentimental humanitarianism, the evolutionary opti-
mists' radiant faith in the future, religious sectarianism, spiritualism, and many other beliefs all have their roots in subjectivity and
are therefore directed primarily to material ends. She does not let
herself be carried away by a philosophy which serves no other
purpose than self-interest, comfort, and well-being. Life means
responsibility and an obligation of involvement and not merely a
naive assumption that any evolutionary development necessarily
means progress in a moral sense. In an essay entitled "Den sterkeste magt" ("The Strongest Power," 1933), she writes: "But the
evolutionary doctrine of the last century, because it regarded evolution as a progressive movement toward something better, and
did not consider that the growth of a cancerous tumor or a paraly-

sis is also evolution, was unconsciously dominated by a medieval religious sentiment." [50] Even Paul Selmer's mother, otherwise a most intelligent woman, expresses such optimism and wishful thinking when she states:

A European war has become an impossibility because the economic life of the different countries has become so interrelated. Besides, the Socialists would be sure to put a stopper on any adventurous policy of that sort—a soldiers' strike would be declared immediately over the whole of Europe. That is precisely Socialism's real contribution to history so far—even now it is a fairly secure guarantee of the world's peace.[51]

It seems to Paul, on the other hand, that the more enlightened people are, the more arbitrary they become, and the more they tend to take the place of God in society.

In another essay entitled "Blasfemi" ("Blasphemy," 1935), Sigrid Undset attacks the spiritualist world of ideas, which is likewise dominated by these same evolutionary dreams. "Like most materialistic idealists or idealistic materialists, the spiritualists assume that in the happy land they envision everyone must find everything he can reasonably demand for his welfare." [52] She concludes: "It is unthinkable that any grown-up human soul that has experienced a personal relation with Him can feel it to be anything but blasphemy when God is reduced to a kind of cornucopia on the top of a sort of cosmic wedding cake." [53] Such concepts of an afterworld can merely bring Christianity into discredit.

In her essay "Reply to a Parish Priest" she acknowledges that greed for personal gain and material enjoyment was prevalent even when the power of the Church was at its highest, but she adds that materialism has never been recognized as an *ideal* in a Catholic community. The present-day belief, however, that those who hold the right religion will certainly receive material benefits on this earth, and that material success is a sure sign of a right religion and of God's special pleasure, she considers the sheer idolatry of the new paganism.[54]

The Catholic veneration of saints stands in direct contrast to the belief in material prosperity and the morality of social respectability. In any other form of hero-worship man sets up figures on pedestals so that he can admire something of himself in them.

Only in the veneration of saints is the cult of success excluded, for with the saints the purpose of life is assessed solely according to spiritual standards.[55]

Sigrid Undset believed that materialism and all other self-centered substitutes for religion must be replaced by the dogmatic authority of the Church; otherwise, man will create political and social ideals in his own image. She writes:

We have no right to assume that any part of European tradition, cultural values, moral concepts, emotional wealth, which has its origin in the dogmatically defined Christianity of the Catholic Church, will continue to live a "natural" life if the people of Europe reject Christianity and refuse to accept God's supernatural grace. One might just as well believe that a tree whose roots are cut off will continue to have leaves and blossoms and fruit.[56]

In the ideologies of materialistic programs and totalitarian movements she saw projections of man's ego divesting itself of the Christian ideal. In a series of essays entitled *Begegnungen und Trennungen* (*Meeting and Parting*), published in Germany in 1931, she makes a distinction between pre-Christian paganism and neo-paganism. "Pre-Christian paganism is a love poem to a God who remained hidden, or it was an attempt to gain the favor of the divine powers whose presence man felt about him. The new paganism is a declaration of war against a God who has revealed himself." [57]

She expresses the same thought in another essay written in German, "Fortschritt, Rasse, Religion" ("Progress, Race, Religion," 1935), this time in direct reference to the Nazi persecution of the Jews. She writes:

The kingdom of God transcends all boundaries of race. It unites all people of the world who are of good will and who have the courage to believe in an eternal life and humble enough to seek fellowship with their Creator instead of the isolation of fetish worship and the cult of self-created things and ideas. This is nothing other than self-worship and this leads to disintegration and death because man cannot exist without supernatural help.[58]

On May 15, 1937, the Norwegian Nazi newspaper, *Fronten*, declared that Sigrid Undset represented one of the most destructive and corrupting forces outside the State, i.e. the Catholic Church.

In 1939 Sigrid Undset wrote another historical novel, *Madame Dorthea*, which has its setting in a remote East Norwegian village in the 1790's. Madame Dorthea is an intelligent and resourceful woman who is faced with the problem of caring for her seven children after the disappearance of her husband under mysterious circumstances. She is a product of eighteenth-century rationalism and its belief that man's moral nature, which is of divine origin, has been revealed to him through the "beautiful light of reason" innate within him. There are, however, inexplicable factors in all existence outside the realm of reason which Madame Dorthea with her rational mind makes every effort to discount, but which she must finally accept as equally fundamental in human affairs.

Unfortunately, the novel was not completed, so that we are unable to follow the further development of Madame Dorthea's character or to see what the future holds in store for her and her children. After the invasion of Norway by the Nazis in 1940 Sigrid Undset was unable to continue work on the novel, nor did she return to this theme after her return from exile five years later. *Madame Dorthea* thus remains her only unfinished novel.

VI *Flight from Norway and Exile (1940–1945)*

On April 7, 1940, Sigrid Undset delivered an address in the Students' Union in Oslo on the topic "Christianity and Our Time." [59] Two days later as she was returning from Mass in St. Olav's Church, the first German airplanes flew over Oslo. She returned to her home at Lillehammer where she had three Finnish refugee children living with her. Her older son Anders joined a machine-gun corps and was killed a few weeks later in the fighting at Segalstad bridge in Gausdal. Her younger son Hans volunteered for service in the Medical Corps. She herself was employed as a censor for a short time at Lillehammer.

On April 20 the Norwegians and the British gave up their positions at Bröttum, south of Lillehammer, and Sigrid Undset was advised to leave her home before the advancing German troops. She had been outspoken in her criticism of Nazism and had taken an active part in helping refugees from Central Europe. Government officials now feared that she might be forced to speak over the German-controlled radio and testify to the "proper behavior" of the Nazis in Norway.

She went north through Gudbrandsdal, and at Hundorp met

some good friends, among them Professor and Mrs. Fredrik
Paasche and their two children. On April 21 she and the Paasches
were at Dombaas when the locality was subjected to a heavy air
attack. Coupled with her great indignation over a bandit's raid
which would destroy everything that the Norwegians had built up
through law and order over a thousand years was her deep love
for her native land. On her flight through Gudbrandsdal she was
deeply moved by the fantastic beauty of Norway's "Valley of Valleys" in the springtime. It seemed incredible to her that anything
so beautiful could be real.[60]

From Dombaas the party traveled to Aandalsnes where they
found the houses aflame on both sides of the main street, and
from there they continued on to Molde and Bud near Hustad-
viken in Romsdal. It was their plan to reach Tromsö in the far
north by fishing boat, but when they were just south of Bodö, they
learned that civilians would not be permitted to land at Tromsö.
Thus they had to retrace their course with another fishing boat
and came south as far as Mo-i-Rana. From here, where the small
party was increased by a group of Norwegian refugees, she made
the hazardous trip over the mountains into Swedish Lapland. It
was rough going for her since she had not been on skis for twenty
years. She was therefore put on a sled with a sick man and drawn
over the mountain road by six young men.

In Stockholm she stayed with a friend and also had the opportunity of seeing her married sister, Mrs. Ragnhild Wiberg. She
recalls the visit late in May to Carl Linné's estate at Hammarby,
near Uppsala. Since earliest youth she had worshiped the great
eighteenth-century naturalist almost as a lay patron saint. As she
kissed the writing desk where his hand had rested so often, she
thought of his words: "The conquered still have a weapon left,
they appeal to God." [61]

In Stockholm she learned of the death of her son Anders and
the surrender of Holland and Belgium. Early in June she was reunited with her younger son Hans, who had been able to make his
escape from Oslo after the capitulation of southern Norway to the
Nazi forces. On June 8 came the news that Norway had been
forced to surrender after a valiant resistance of sixty days. Before
the beginning of hostilities Sigrid Undset had made arrangements
to travel to the United States on a lecture tour. She now felt the
time had come to fulfill this obligation.

On July 13 she and Hans flew to Moscow, and after a stay of four days in the Russian capital they continued on a nine-day journey with the Trans-Siberian Railroad to Vladivostok and then to Kobe, Japan.[62]

Nothing that she saw in Russia could awaken a sympathetic response in her. Everywhere she found poverty and human suffering, squalor and filth. The war against Finland had proved that Russia had a powerful modern army, but she believed that the time would certainly come when Russia would have to admit openly that it was a "nationalistic and imperialistic state system, ruled by a clique under the thumb of Joseph Stalin." [63]

By contrast with Russia she found Japan clean and attractive. The people were peace-loving except for the small group of warlords whom she held responsible for the country's policy of war and conquest.[64] Above all, she had a real understanding for the Japanese people and their belief in the spiritual reality behind the phenomenal world.

From Kobe she and her son sailed for the United States on the *President Cleveland*, arriving in San Francisco on August 26. From there she went to New York, where she was scheduled to give a series of lectures.[65] She stayed for a short time in the Algonquin Hotel on 44th Street and then rented an apartment in the Columbia Heights section of Brooklyn, possibly because from that vantage point she could see Norwegian ships lying at anchor. She traveled extensively during the five years of her exile in the United States, spending several summers in Monterey in western Massachusetts and visiting Willa Cather in upper New York State and Marjorie Kinnan Rawlings in Florida. Seven times she crossed the United States from coast to coast.

In a series of essays written during her stay in the United States, Sigrid Undset has given her impressions of the beauty of the land [66] and of the friendliness and helpfulness of the men and women she met.[67] She pays a stirring tribute to the American way of life and the tradition of freedom passed on to later generations by America's founding fathers.[68]

She wrote numerous book reviews for *The New York Times* and *The New York Herald-Tribune* and contributed to various anthologies, but literature was far from her thoughts at this time. She had no plans to return to her unfinished novel *Madame Dorthea*, but was merely interested in "writing propaganda," as she remarked when interviewed soon after arrival.

She forgot the artist's detachment when she wrote of Germany. She hated the Nazi catchwords about blood and race and denied that the Germans were racial kinsmen of the Norwegians. With Norway's conversion to Christianity serfdom had been abolished and the rights of the individual as a free man recognized, but the Germans had now reversed the process and made thralls out of the Norwegians.[69] She railed against the pro-Nazi Norwegians who sold their land in order to be a dictator's lapdogs.[70] Norway had thought it would be able to preserve its neutrality, but it was not a nation of cowards merely because its people had become peace-loving. In 1814 the Norwegians proved that they could fight in their struggle for freedom and independence, and in April, 1940, poorly trained and inadequately equipped soldiers struggled with the courage of lions for sixty days in attempting to defend their country against the invaders.[71] She writes: "It was Hitler's mistake not to believe that democracies were prepared to fight for their lives and the right to continue to live as democracies, but it was our mistake not to realize that some nations truly could believe in war as a means to progress and prosperity." [72]

The intensity of Sigrid Undset's bitterness against the Germans is understandable; she had seen her country invaded and one of her sons killed in the war, and now she was a homeless exile facing an uncertain future. However, overshadowing her own personal loss, was her concern for the fate of free people in the ideological confrontation of democracies with the totalitarian states. In the past some civilized peoples have been almost eradicated from the surface of the earth, but in the face of danger they have always been able to muster reserves and preserve remnants of their culture. The difficulties of communication then prevailing prevented destructive forces from spreading themselves over larger areas, so that good was able to exist beside evil. Today, however, the world has become much smaller and no nation can isolate itself from others, so that there is nothing to prevent a wave of destruction from inundating our whole world.[73]

Sigrid Undset had always rejected all materialistic and mechanistic philosophies which, by abolishing God and erecting man as the measure of all things, are without metaphysical basis. For the same reason she rejected all Fascist and Communist ideologies as mere projections of the human ego. In totalitarian states the individual disclaims all sense of responsibility and ignores any obligation above self-interest. He is given what he seeks, but at the price of his own personal freedom. Deprived of all compulsion, either for good or evil, he becomes a slave of the State with no freedom of will. But Christianity has taught that man is of divine origin and destiny, that he belongs to the supernatural world of the spirit and that he has rights as an individual, but also obligations to others. In a world beset with dangers and temptations, free will can be a dangerous gift and a burden, but "since man is endowed with reason and freedom he is able to interpret the universe and his place in it and is made responsible for all that he does, and capable of endless growth through the right use of freedom." [74]

In her essay "Progress, Race, Religion" and also in a second essay, "Brorskapets religion" ("The Religion of Brotherhood," 1948), published after her return to Norway, she writes of the Christian concept of brotherhood:

Biological kinship is certainly the source of the strongest and most dependable love between human beings. But however dependable it may be, it still has its limitations.—The fact is that with Christianity another kind of brotherhood enters the world, a brotherhood among all men who believe that we have a Father in Heaven and that His word has become flesh, Jesus, the first-born of all brothers. With this the words brother and brotherhood have been given new meaning.[75]

Sigrid Undset also found time to write the introduction to twelve stories of Steen Steensen Blicher, translated from the Danish by Hanna Astrup Larsen. Blicher had always been one of her favorite writers, and when her first book *Mrs. Marta Oulie* was published in 1907, her mother gave her a copy of Blicher's *Trækfuglene* (*Birds of Passage*) with the dedication: "As a writer you will always look up to Steen Blicher as your model, for profound integrity, fearless acceptance of life as it is, and truthfulness in telling what you know." [76]

While in the United States Sigrid Undset wrote several children's books in English, one of which, the aforementioned *Happy Days in Norway* (1942), was later translated into Norwegian as *Lykkelige dager* (1947). Mrs. Eleanor Roosevelt had suggested that refugee authors from occupied countries should describe what life was like for the children of their homelands before the Germans marched in. It was her belief that American children, informed of the practices and customs of children in other lands, would be better prepared in the future to build bridges of friendship and understanding among the nations of the world. After Sigrid Undset had read several such accounts, including one about Czechoslovakia, she agreed to write a comparable one about the children of Norway. She tells of what was probably the happiest time of her life, the years spent in her home "Bjerkebæk" at Lillehammer, when amid the most pleasant surroundings she was able to produce her best work and at the same time have the necessary time to devote herself to the care and happiness of her three children and her many friends. At home in Norway she had tried to shield her family from the many reporters and strangers who flocked to Lillehammer after her fame had spread beyond the borders of her own country. Now she opens the doors of "Bjerkebæk" and shares with the reader all her precious memories of the home which she might never see again and of her children, only one of whom was still living. She is able to forget her own personal grief, for she writes with great warmth of feeling, with humor and with a smile, but it is a smile which shines through tears.

She also published in English another children's story, *Sigurd and His Brave Companions* (1943), which she had written originally in German as *Die Saga von Vilmund Vidutan und seinen Gefährten* (1931).[77] Herein with simple humor she tells of three young boys from seven to twelve years of age who act out the mighty exploits of Vilmund, the hero of a saga as related to them by their parish priest. The fourteenth-century tale has something of the life and vigor of the age of Haakon V, but its strength lies in the realistic description of energetic and mischievous boys with wholesome imaginations. Sigrid Undset also relates how the boys are instructed by their parish priest, who tells them something of Jesus and His mother Mary, of the wisdom of the apostles and of the unfailing courage of the Christian martyrs.

She returned to one of her greatest interests when she wrote the introduction to a selection of the folk tales of Asbjörnsen and Moe entitled *True and Untrue and Other Norse Tales* (1945).[78] With sound scholarship and mastery of material she gives an account of the origins, themes, and character of the old tales, their migration from country to country and their importance as social and historical records. She also calls attention to the moral nature of the Norwegian folk tales: the good and the brave are always rewarded and the wicked receive their just deserts. She finds these tales realistic and down-to-earth, for she writes:

Although the Norwegian folk tales have wandered far and wide through space and time, to us Norwegians they seem to be blood of our own blood and bone of our own bone, as homely as our mountains and forests and fjords. They express our way of looking at life and judging people. We never liked glamor, we always thought it rather vulgar—real life with its troubles and jokes and sorrows and joys were good enough for us, and even when we daydreamed, we dreamed of a world not too unlike the one we knew and loved.[79]

For the United States Government Sigrid Undset prepared a cultural index of Norway, a listing of all monuments, relics, buildings, churches, museums, etc.[80] With her encyclopedic knowledge, power of memory, and her love of her native land she was perhaps better equipped than anyone else to prepare such an inventory.

A valuable selection of her essays, composed for the most part of those written during her five years in the United States, was edited and published after her death by Professor A. H. Winsnes, in 1952.[81]

In February, 1942, Sigrid Undset received an honorary degree from Rollins College, and in May, 1943, she was likewise honored by Smith College. The latter citation reads: "One of the great novelists of our time, whose works have reached a public extending far beyond the boundaries of Norway, because her characters, whether drawn from the past or the present life of her country, are the progeny of common humanity, and in their somber grandeur reveal her deep understanding of the tragic lot of us all. She has done much to make her country and her people part of the cultural heritage of the civilized world. Symbol of the magnificent struggle which the Norwegian people, against fearful odds, continue to wage indomitably for their freedom and ours." [82]

In August, 1945, she returned to Norway on the freighter *Montevideo* and again took up residence in her home at Lillehammer.

On her 65th birthday, May 20, 1947, the Grand Cross of the Order of St. Olav was conferred upon her by King Haakon VII. She was the first woman after Crown Princess Märtha to be so honored and was particularly gratified that this recognition came to her not for her literary fame, but for service to her country in its struggle for freedom.

During the last years of her life she wrote a biography of Catherine of Siena, the great fourteenth-century Church reformer and revered saint of the Dominicans. This work, published posthumously, draws a convincing portrait of the psychological and religious development of a woman so far removed from our own times, but formed like Sigrid Undset in a heroic mold and thus so appealing to the modern reader.

She continued to write for newspapers and periodicals, but the war, the pressure of work, and her personal grief had begun to take their inevitable toll. After her return from the United States she no longer had her former energy and unflagging spirit. Her sister, Mrs. Signe Undset Thomas, has informed me that she suffered severely from bronchitis and a persistent cough which grew progressively worse. There is a note of resignation and disappointment in a letter she wrote to the author Hans Aanrud on December 20, 1948.

I can indeed say that I think the world has become dismal. During the war, when I was in America, I had the feeling that I was making myself useful and that we could all look to the future with some kind of hopeful expectation. Not that I expected everything to become excellent all of a sudden, or that "the good old days" should return. But neither did I expect "the new age" to be so anemic and feeble, although with so much blood spilled it is not strange that people should suddenly give the impression of being anemic, rebellious, and unenterprising.[83]

Sigrid Undset died at Lillehammer on June 10, 1949. In her typewriter at the time of her death was the manuscript of an article on Edmund Burke, the great British statesman of the eighteenth century, like herself an apostle of freedom. As a token of the high esteem in which Norway held its gifted writer, she was buried with great honors at Mesnalien, the churchyard near Lillehammer. There she rests, like Kristin Lavransdatter, a "loyal handmaiden of the Lord," between her older son Anders, who gave his life for his country, and her daughter, Maren Charlotte, whose life was another kind of holocaust. The stark black cross which marks her grave is a fitting symbol of the straightness and strength of her life.

CHAPTER 2

Early Works

I Mrs. Marta Oulie

SIGRID UNDSET'S first work, *Mrs. Marta Oulie* (1907), is a short novel written in diary form. From various entries we learn that Marta has become involved in an affair with Henrik, her husband's "best friend." When Otto Oulie is stricken with tuberculosis and brought to a sanatorium, Marta feels the full impact of the transgression through which she has ruined her whole life. Otto dies without suspecting any wrong-doing on Marta's part, but she is now so consumed with remorse and self-reproach that she is unwilling and unable to accept her lover's offer of marriage.

As mentioned above, for the liberally-oriented Norwegian society at the beginning of the twentieth century there was nothing particularly new in such a story of marital infidelity. In Sigrid Undset's novel, however, one finds no trace of the sordidness usually associated with the treatment of this theme. Much more important to the young author is a description of the self-analysis to which Marta subjects herself in her attempt to account for her complete failure in life. Through the skillful use of flashbacks Sigrid Undset opens the curtain of the past to reveal Marta as a young student who is seemingly interested in the question of women's rights and involved in various programs of social and political reform. However, like all young women in Sigrid Undset's novels, Marta also dreams of love and happiness, so that all other interests are quickly relegated to the background as soon as she meets Otto Oulie, a handsome young businessman and outdoor enthusiast who radiates good health and vitality. Marta writes: "This was fresh air and sunshine which came into my room where I sat over my books. God knows how glad I was to throw away the books and run out into the bright world." [1]

Marta and Otto are extremely happy during their courtship and

55

the first years of their married life. Although Marta is intellectually superior to the somewhat unimaginative Otto, there is every
indication that the marriage is most successful. Otto is a devoted
husband and father whose only concern is the welfare of his family, and Marta for her part now sees her fondest wishes realized in
the establishment of a home with husband and children. Her happiness, however, is based entirely on the absolute devotion and
boundless love which she expects of Otto, for love is Marta's
greatest need. She writes that it is the only thing in life which is of
any value, for "there is no soul outside the life of our bodies—it
lives in us like a flame in something that is burning. Each day I
felt how it was making me beautiful and fresh and radiant, how it
gave me understanding of life and made me brave and gay and
infinitely superior." [2]

Though Marta readily accepts Otto's love, she is nevertheless so
enmeshed in the web of her own egoism and self-worship that she
cannot appreciate the finer qualities of her husband's character.
Otto's only thoughts are for his wife and their three children. It
does not occur to him that Marta might not love home and family
as deeply as he. The routine life of the housewife soon begins to
pall on Marta. She feels that she has sacrificed too many of her
own interests for the sake of this marriage and even seems to begrudge Otto the happiness that he finds in his home. She derives
no joy or comfort from her children. She thinks she has done
enough for them in providing them with food and clothing; yet
she is surprised and hurt that they feel themselves more closely
attached to Otto than to her.

When the heady wine of her romantic love has worn off, an
insatiable desire drives her into an affair with Henrik. However,
for Marta there is no happiness to be found in this liaison. She
readily admits that she cared no more for Henrik than for "the
mirror on her dresser," [3] and what he might suffer from this affair
was of no concern to her. The fact is that Marta in her self-
infatuation and complete indifference to the welfare of others has
completely isolated herself from all other human beings and is
thus incapable of experiencing any true love, whether it be with
Otto or Henrik or anyone else.

Not until her husband becomes ill does she begin to see the
error of her ways. Then she finally realizes that she had merely
wanted Otto to think her beautiful, to kiss her and grant her every

wish. "Never did I try to discover his true self and give it under-standing and love." [4] She has likewise been selfish in her attitude toward others outside the family, for she has always judged people by appearances and not by their inner worth. Now she learns that no human life can exist in a vacuum: each individual derives his strength from others and in return he must reach out and give of himself for the welfare of his fellow men.

An earlier conversation between Marta and Otto throws some light on the religious beliefs of the young couple. Marta is an athe-ist who believes neither in God nor in a life hereafter. For her, the world is too unjust to inspire faith in a personal God. God must be a slave driver if he subdues the obstinate by imposing on them a life of great trials. Otto, on the other hand, has an abiding faith in a divine authority. He views the teaching of the Bible with some skepticism because he will not simply accept on faith alone what the pastors teach. However, one has the feeling that he lets his "healthy reason" speak, merely in order not to appear too naive to his fiancée, for when faced with death, Otto finds peace of mind in the religious faith of his childhood. He places his trust in "Someone" who is both strong and merciful, and he dies with the assurance that he and Marta will meet again in another life.

Marta, on the other hand, does not have such Christian faith in which to find solace. She has always relied completely on her own strength and considered herself equal to any exigencies with which she might be confronted. In her diary she writes:

I once said that I could commit murder and continue to live with my conscience as a witness and judge and be prepared to accept either punishment or pardon. My God, here I just go about wondering whether I can confess to anyone and I lie awake at night thinking about that.[5]

She refuses to accept her husband's faith but she can understand the solace confession must bring.

Marta has the intellect to understand the inner logic of Christi-anity. She writes:

Seen from the inside, Christianity is consistent enough—it is as though one were standing in a lofty cathedral with stained-glass windows. If it only were not for the fact that the whole real world and the daylight are outside! [6]

Marta would like to find release from her cares in an all-embracing faith, but she finds it impossible to reconcile a belief in an eternal God and the remission of sin through divine grace with her own sad fate. She prefers to remain outside the cathedral, but there she finds herself alone, for the world she thinks is so real is merely the reflection of her own image.

II The Happy Age

Den lykkelige alder (*The Happy Age*), which was published in 1908, includes two sketches, "Et halvt dusin lommetørklær" ("A Half Dozen Handkerchiefs") and "Dröm" ("Dream"), and two short stories, *En fremmed* (*A Stranger*) and *The Happy Age*. It is from the last of these stories that the book takes its title.

In this collection Sigrid Undset reveals much more of her childhood and adolescent experiences than in *Mrs. Marta Oulie*. The title itself is ironical, for it reflects merely the image of happy and carefree youth which mothers and aunts have constructed in their own minds without an understanding for the heartaches and disappointments that young girls so often suffer.

There is a bitter-sweet quality to the sketch "Dream." Here Sigrid Undset attempts to analyse the meaning of dreams she had had as a child of ten years and again as a young girl of sixteen. In "A Half Dozen Handkerchiefs" little Bildit is a pathetic figure in the way she accepts disappointment without even a murmur. Early in life she has learned that poor children must do without much that the parents of other children can afford. She is able to bear the pain of this hardship, but in order to avoid embarrassment and the loss of face with her schoolmates she follows her natural instinct in resorting to little lies.

In the two short stories, *A Stranger* and *The Happy Age*, Sigrid Undset introduces a number of young women of the type with which she became acquainted during her ten years of office employment (1899–1909). They are self-supporting girls who come from good middle-class families, but who are now removed from the shelter of the home. They live in drab rented rooms or boardinghouses and work in shops and offices. They seem to derive no great joy from their employment or from their newly-won independence. Proud and reserved beneath a cool exterior these young girls are warmhearted and they dream of a love worthy of their complete surrender. They are of fine moral character, but often

they become disillusioned and depressed, and in the conflict between dream and reality they are forced to compromise with their
ideals. Despite many characteristics which these girls have in
common, they are all vividly conceived and presented as complete
personalities.

One of the loveliest of these young women is Edele Hammer in
the story *A Stranger*. She is the daughter of a Swedish mother and
a Norwegian father, both now dead. Although born and brought
up in Oslo, Edele has never considered herself anything but a
stranger in the Norwegian capital. Because of her reserved nature
she finds it difficult to establish any close friendships with the
young people she meets in her boardinghouse or the office where
she is employed. She finds distasteful all tales of casual love
affairs, the constant topic of conversation among her acquaint-
ances. Often she asks herself: "How can any woman do such a
thing?" However, she refrains from all criticism, for she adds:
"Can any of us be certain how pure we wanted to be when we
first joined in the game?" [7]

Edele does join in the game when she becomes involved in a
love affair with a young engineer, Alf Aagaard. Her love for Alf is
not a selfish one, like that of Marta Oulie, but a love born of pity
and sympathy for the erratic and unstable youth. She soon becomes disillusioned with Alf and breaks with him, but the experience leaves deep scars. She now feels unworthy of the love which
an old friend, the architect Per Dyrssen, is prepared to offer her.
She believes she has no right to intrude upon his world of peace
and contentment, for she has nothing with which to repay him for
his love.

Per, however, understands how much she has suffered and
through his kindness is able to raise her from the slough of her
despondency. He too has known loneliness and needs Edele's love
to make his own life complete. Edele believes in him, for he offers
her a handful of real stars from heaven and not a bit of "elfin gold
which turns to withered leaves with the coming of daylight." [8]
Above all, he breaks through the shell of isolation in which she
has concealed herself and which has been the cause of her unhap-
piness. He teaches her that true happiness is to be found in association with others and concern for their interests. With all the
warmth of her heart Edele has nevertheless always been so self-
contained that she has been unable to reveal to others her true

feelings, and for the same reason has been unwilling to accept acts
of kindness when offered in a true spirit of friendship. In his
hands Per holds the stars from heaven, but it remains for Edele to
reach out and grasp them. We sense that Edele has been given a
better understanding of true human values through Per's love and
that she now will no longer be "a stranger" as before.

The two central figures of the second story, *The Happy Age*, are
Charlotte Hedels and Uni Hirsch. Of all the characters in Sigrid
Undset's contemporary novels, Charlotte reveals most clearly the
author's preoccupation with the problems confronting the young
working girls in Oslo in the early years of the twentieth century.
Charlotte is an office worker, but she dreams of becoming an author and writing realistic fiction according to a program which
corresponds precisely to that pursued so consistently by Sigrid
Undset in her early works. Indeed, we catch an echo of the author's very own words as Charlotte speaks to her friend Uni:

I wanted to write about the town. You know, all these gloomy districts
we respectable drudges live in. The wet dirty streets with their worn
pavements and small apartments and little shops. I should like to write
about the windows of such shops—shops with toilet articles, toy shops
with dolls and sewing boxes and necklaces of glass beads, where children stand outside in clusters and pick out what they would like best.
When I just think of how many small yearnings are fixed on each of
these poor treasures! . . . I should like to make use of all the worn-out
little words we let fall so carelessly—words with which we hurt one
another, words we utter as a little expression of love, words we whisper
to people in their sadness or with which we surprise them in moments
of happiness. . . . I could write a book about you or about myself or
about any of us poor office slaves. We carry on with our work; it gives
us something to live from, but we can't live *for* it.[9]

Even though Charlotte lives at home with her widowed mother
and two sisters, she feels intensely the loneliness of her entire existence. Tensions arise at home because her mother, devoted as
she is, has no understanding for the real cause of Charlotte's grief
—her longing to free herself from the narrow circle of her meaningless little world with its boredom and frustrations and to have
life begin to unfold in all its rich abundance.

Charlotte's poetry reveals a mood of abject despondency which
is even more intense than that of Sigrid Undset's early verse col-

lection *Ungdom (Youth)*.[10] Whereas the melancholy which pervades the author's youthful poems is at times alleviated by an almost mystical longing for something infinite to worship, Charlotte feels that she has been completely forgotten in a world where she has ceased to exist.

As yet Charlotte has found nothing in life worthy of such worship. She says to Uni:

We all want the same thing, whatever way we choose to get it: to live for one moment with our whole being turned inward, so that our eyes do not look out into the fog and gaslights, but into our own burning hearts.[11]

For such girls there is nothing in life which can hold their interest once they come home from office or shop or school. So they walk alone and dream their little dreams. For them life is a spiritual vacuum with no chance for any change, and because they find no response to their yearning they become, as Uni remarks, "like Narcissus, who became enamored of his own reflection and drowned."[12]

Charlotte takes her own life because she has been unable to reconcile her dreams with the harsh facts of reality. Like Narcissus she too is enamored of her own image and unable to find anything of value in life beyond herself.

There is likewise much of this self-worship to be found in Uni Hirsch who comes from the same impecunious middle-class background as Charlotte Hedels. However, whereas Charlotte is introspective and given to moods of despondency, Uni is lively and gay. She longs for the many nice things which money can buy and therefore she feels the pinch of poverty all the more. Her aspirations of becoming an actress are encouraged by friends, and she is fortunate enough in having the opportunity of appearing on the stage on several occasions, even though only in plays of minor importance. Attractive and with a pleasing voice and sufficient dramatic ability she enjoys a modest degree of success.

However, Uni becomes engaged to Kristian Hjelde, a young engineer, whose vision of a home and family does not include a wife performing in the theater. At the same time he is realist enough to understand that Uni's devotion to her art may be even greater than her love for him. The only reality for Uni is her yearning for the development of her own personality and the pursuit of her career. Kristian does not offer Uni any encouragement, because deep in his heart he doubts whether she possesses the necessary talent to make a success of a career on the stage. On the other hand, he does not discourage her either. He even refuses to accept a position in a small provincial town, although it offers the promise of more rapid promotion, because he does not wish to deprive Uni of the opportunity of appearing on the stage in Oslo.

It is Uni, however, and not Kristian, who must make the final decision, for her initial success as an actress is followed by disappointment and failure. Only then does she begin to appreciate the true meaning of all Kristian's efforts to protect her and to establish a home built upon a solid foundation of love and mutual understanding. She marries Kristian and thus renounces the theater once and for all and with it all hopes of realizing the fulfillment of her romantic dream. Such happiness in marriage would have been everything Charlotte Hedels could have asked for. Uni, however, is cast of another mold; it is difficult for her to forget herself for someone else. When her first child is born, she feels that she is now tied forever to a home and to children that she feels belong only to her husband. Limited financial resources and the drudgery of housework contribute to the irritation and tension between Kristian and herself. Uni believes that by renouncing her own dreams of happiness she has sacrificed too much on the altar of marriage, for there is still some longing in her soul which will never be answered in Kristian Hjelde's home. "But no one shall ever know about this," she whispers to her infant daughter.[13] In the story *Mrs. Hjelde*, which Sigrid Undset wrote as a sequel to *The Happy Age*, we learn whether Uni is able to carry out her good intention of suppressing her own personal desires and of finding a lasting happiness in a mother's devotion and care for her home and family.

III   Gunnar's Daughter

In her autobiographical reminiscences, *The Longest Years*, Sigrid Undset tells of the discovery of a copy of *Njál's Saga* in the library of her paternal grandfather at Vollan near Trondheim, and how thrilled she was to read of the daring exploits of Njál's brave but erratic and unstable son Skarphedin.[14] In the essay "En bok som blev et vendepunkt i mitt liv" ("A Book that Was a Turning

Point in My Life"), she likewise recalls how this same saga
opened up for her a completely new world, that of medieval Iceland and the fascinating genre of the Icelandic family saga.[15] She
was particularly impressed by the moral conflict with which men
of the saga age were confronted. She noticed how often the hero
of an Icelandic family saga was torn between the dictates of his
heart and his sense of moral right and the obligation which he
owed to his nearest kin. The family unit, far from being a source
of strength, actually set restrictions upon an individual's freedom
of action and consequently placed him in a dilemma from which
he was unable to extricate himself.

In *The Longest Years* Sigrid Undset also relates that during the
last days of her father's illness she used to read aloud to him selections from the Old Icelandic sagas. She could not understand the
Old Norse of the *Elder Edda*, but the late romantic poems and
many prose sagas such as the *Hervarar Saga* were not beyond her.
Her father was always ready to help by explaining some strange
grammatical construction or a train of thought that people followed in old days.[16] Her antiquarian interests, particularly in the
field of Scandinavian history and literature, had been kindled very
early in life by her learned father, so that it may not seem too
surprising that after her first novels of contemporary life she
should return to that period of Scandinavia's past which so greatly
stirred her imagination.

Fortellingen om Viga-Ljot og Vigdis (tr. as *Gunnar's Daughter*, 1909) is a grim medieval romance which has its setting in the
eleventh century when Christianity had as yet made little
impression on the minds of men in this early family society. It was
a time when the ethical principle of revenge determined men's
actions, and it is this spirit of unrelenting hatred and thirst for
vengeance which serves as the central theme of this saga.

Ljot, an Icelander, on a trading voyage to Norway, takes lodg-
ing with Gunnar at his farmstead on the Oslo Fjord. Here he
meets Vigdis, the daughter of Gunnar, whom he would gladly win
as his wife. To Vigdis it soon becomes apparent that the young
Icelander is impetuous and hotheaded, and she requests a certain
period of time before she can make any decision.

Vigdis is a pagan priestess who makes sacrifice to the gods of
her ancestors in a sacred grove. However, she is beginning to be
of the same mind as her father, who has given up the old faith and

puts his whole trust in his own power and strength. Ljot, to be
sure, is a Christian, but not out of any conviction. He had let
himself be baptized at the request of a pious recluse in Denmark
who healed a gangrenous wound and who would accept no other
reward for his help.

There is good reason to believe that Vigdis returns Ljot's love
and in due time would probably have accepted him in marriage,
but Ljot acts unwisely on numerous occasions and does not sue
for her hand in honorable fashion. Instead, he violates her and
returns to Iceland, but not before he is forced to hear Vigdis vent
her wrath upon him with the curse: "May you have the worst of
deaths—and live long and miserably—you and all you hold dear.
And may you see your children die a most wretched death before
your eyes." [17]

Upon his return to Iceland Ljot marries Leikny, who bears him
four children, but the memory of Vigdis, whom he still loves so
dearly, casts a shadow over the marriage. His enemies learn the
reason for his silence and sullenness and quickly spread the tale of
his rejection by Vigdis. In an unguarded moment Leikny hears
from Ljot's own lips that he will grieve, as long as he lives, that he
possessed and yet lost a fair maid in Norway. All four children of
Leikny and Ljot die in their earliest years; Ljot himself is a witness to the tragic death of two of his children by drowning.
Leikny cannot recover from the shock of this loss and dies in
Ljot's arms. Ljot's youngest son is a malformed weakling, but because he is a Christian, Ljot refuses to follow the pagan custom of
exposing the child to die. However, this boy, too, soon dies and
Ljot feels that he has received his just punishment for the wrong
he has done Vigdis, whose prayer of vengeance has now been
answered.

In Norway Vigdis gives birth to Ljot's son and out of hatred for
Ljot abandons the child in the woods to die. The child, however,
is saved by one of her thralls, and Vigdis now sees in the child the
proper instrument of her revenge. To her foster-mother she says:
"That would be my best revenge, if Ljot's son were to become
Ljot's slayer. Not lightly would he escape from the dog I reared
with hate and blows, until he had his teeth in Viga-Ljot's
throat." [18]

On another occasion, too, Vigdis reveals the same relentless
fury of her hate. Eyjolf, a rejected suitor, has slandered Vigdis,

and in an attempt to avenge the insult to his daughter Gunnar has received a mortal wound at the hands of Eyjolf. Demanding a life for a life Vigdis strikes stealthily as soon as night falls. While Eyjolf sleeps, she thrusts a knife into his heart, well aware of the fact that she is doing violence to a man no more able to defend himself against her than she had been against Ljot. Because of this slaying she is forced to leave her home and flee with her young son through the forest in the bitter cold of winter. As she looks back, she sees a red glare in the sky above her home and she knows that Koll, Eyjolf's brother, has put the torch to her farmstead.

She finds refuge in the hut of three outlaws and remains with them until she has the opportunity of presenting her case before King Olav Tryggvason, who is active in preaching the new faith in Norway and friendly toward all who will become Christians. King Olav helps the three outlaws make their peace and grants Vigdis protection and safe-conduct home. In return she allows herself and her son to be baptized. She gives the boy the name Ulvar ("Wolf"), because she carried him that night through the wolves' forest.

Upon her return home proper reparation is made to Vigdis for the destruction of her farmstead. She has her houses rebuilt and a church constructed of good timber. However, she is not very zealous in the faith, for her sole concern is to prepare Ljot's son for the revenge she so craves. It is her fondest wish that Ulvar bring her Ljot's head and place it in her lap. Illugi, one of the outlaws who had aided Vigdis in her flight through the woods and who now trains Ulvar in the use of arms, remarks to her: "Your love for this Ljot must have been great, because you still hate him so fiercely— I almost think you still love him." [19] And so it is, for like Gudrun in the *Laxdoela Saga* and possibly Hallgerd in *Njál's Saga* so too can Vigdis say: "I could not have hated him so long. The worst thing of all was that he was the man I would have wished to love above all others." [20]

On a Viking expedition off the coast of Scotland, Ulvar is hard pressed by the enemy and manages to escape with his life only with the help of Ljot who arrives on the scene at the most crucial moment. Together they return to Norway where Ulvar learns the identity of the man he has come to love and admire. To Vigdis, however, Ljot's return means only that the game between them may now be played out to a conclusion after these many years. She incites Ulvar to the deed of vengeance, but in the duel which ensues he flinches from striking any serious blow, torn as he is between his love for his father and his duty toward his mother. In his feeling of guilt Ljot actually inflicts a mortal wound upon himself and as he dies, he says: "But do not grieve over this; for it was my own wish, that it should end this way. My son, may God grant that you not inherit our fortunes. Now do as your mother wishes; long have I yearned that my head might lie in her lap." [21]

To Vigdis finally comes the vengeance long after the desire for it has disappeared. The wretched gray head that Ulvar lays heavily in her lap is no atonement for her many long years of misfortune and suffering. She has Ljot buried outside the church which she had built after her conversion. After ten more years, during which she sits alone and will see no one, Vigdis dies and is buried near another church, one dedicated to Saint Margaret.

In *Gunnar's Daughter* Sigrid Undset has made an attempt to imitate the style and spirit of the Old Icelandic saga. The tale reflects all the stark violence consistent with the spirit of this early Christian period. In the silent fortitude with which she faces adversity, Vigdis is a woman of heroic grandeur, but she displays a relentless fury in the manner in which she carries out her vengeance to the grave. Despite the slightly conciliatory tone of the conclusion, Christianity had made no impression upon the minds of the principal characters of this tale. The world of dark violence is relieved but little by the humanity and understanding which Sigrid Undset shows in her later works.

In imitating the style of the saga Sigrid Undset has been only moderately successful. The Icelandic saga writers present the external facts in a clear and lucid style and let the reader draw his own conclusions from the circumstances as described. Character is revealed through the subtle technique of understatement and through terse utterances and cutting rejoinders rather than through psychological analysis. In this way the author does not intrude upon the scene of action nor does he permit himself to make any moral judgments. Sigrid Undset attempts to observe a certain epic objectivity, but it is difficult for her with her great love for detail to adapt herself to the rigid limitations of such a style. As a woman of strong imagination and feeling she looks into the hearts of her characters. Behind the facts she sees human relationships where others see only drab details. *Gunnar's Daughter* is a tale written from a woman's point of view, and many of its passages, charged with emotion, are conceived in a style completely foreign to the saga. This genre did not allow Sigrid Undset the proper freedom which she needed in order to make full use of all her knowledge of the Middle Ages and to unfold a tapestry which depicts so brilliantly the atmosphere and color of bygone times. It was in her medieval novels that she was to find the proper vehicle for her narrative and expository talents.

CHAPTER 3

Social Novels

I Jenny

JENNY, Sigrid Undset's first full-length novel, was written during the summer of 1911, after she had returned from her stay
in Italy and France. Oslo is again the setting for a considerable
portion of the novel, but this time the oppressive atmosphere of
the city's middle-class milieu stands in sharp contrast to the colorful and stimulating background of Rome and the beauty of the
Campagna in the springtime, as described in the early part of the
novel.

Jenny, a young woman of twenty-eight, has achieved some success as a painter and has gone to Rome to perfect her art. Freed
from the distractions and responsibilities weighing upon her at
home, she is able to give undivided attention to her work and
at the same time enjoy life in the congenial company of a few
Scandinavian friends. A gentle and lovable young woman, she en-
lists our sympathies. In contrast to the flightiness of her friend
Cesca, she is serious-minded and determined to surmount all ob-
stacles in order to maintain her independence of spirit. She has
had a difficult youth and like many young people of her generation has started life stripped of all illusions. She has seen, however, that many people have the strength to conquer despite ad-
verse circumstances and have the courage to struggle on without
allowing themselves to be degraded or debased, and this observa-
tion is enough to make her optimistic. She has complete faith in
herself and a strict moral code which rejects casual liaisons and
the belief that sexual license is proper and good merely because it
reflects man's natural instincts. She says: "I believe in my dreams;
I will call nothing happiness unless it is the happiness I longed
for, and I still believe such happiness exists. If it is not to be mine,
then it will be my own fault. It will be because I have been one of

the foolish virgins who did not watch and wait for the bride-groom." [1]

Until this time Jenny has been able to control her emotions and impulses, but now she begins to experience a growing emptiness in her life and a feeling of isolation. She has not been able to find a synthesis between the pleasure and joy derived from her art and her woman's nature. She realizes that women can never reach the point where their work means everything to them. She longs for the love of a man whom she can prize higher than herself. She will not be reckless with her love; from sheer sensual satisfaction she will not throw herself into the arms of any man who might enter her life at some crucial moment. "The joy she longed for should be fiery and consuming, but it should also be spotlessly clean. She would be loyal and true to the man to whom she gave herself, but he would have to take her completely, so that not a single possibility in her would be wasted or left neglected in some corner of her soul." [2]

Helge Gram, a young Norwegian student of archeology who has just arrived in Rome, is not the man who can fill this position in Jenny's life. Though more intelligent than Alf Aagaard of the story *A Stranger*, he is just as immature and neurotic and in addition is bound by emotional ties to his mother. Jenny has a limited sympathy for him, especially because he is so unsure of himself in these new surroundings, and offers him the same kindness and friendship which she is accustomed to give to all who depend upon her. The awkward youth, appealing to her maternal feelings, declares his love, and Jenny, tossed as she is between moods and desires, allows herself to drift into an engagement, even though her deeper feelings are not involved.

Most heroines in Sigrid Undset's novels are able to adjust themselves to new situations, but Jenny is a sensitive person who looks upon the engagement as a betrayal of her better self. She lied to herself in thinking that she was prepared to share the intensity of Helge's love, and now she finds it humiliating to have given promises which she feels she cannot keep.

The relationship deteriorates when the young couple returns to Oslo. Here Jenny is introduced to Helge's father and mother, who live in Welhaven Street, for Sigrid Undset one of the most depressing streets in the city and the one which best typifies the middle-class society she so detested. Helge's mother is of a distrustful and suspicious nature and reveals her instinctive hatred of Jenny at their first meeting. Much to her own dismay Jenny is caught up in the web of falsehoods and deceitful practices which seem to be quite common in this household. In this milieu Helge again becomes the victim of his mother's domineering influence from which he was beginning to free himself while in Rome. Helge and Jenny make every effort to cling to what they call their love but what is really nothing more than the memory of a few romantic dreams far removed from present reality. The engagement is broken off after the vulgarity and jealousy of Helge's mother has led to many unpleasant scenes that are more than Jenny's sensitive feelings can endure.

The experience has left deep scars on Jenny's soul, for she believes that in her relations with Helge she has been guilty of the same levity she has always hated in other women. She therefore welcomes the consolation which Gert Gram, Helge's father, can give her. He tries to convince her that it was only a temporary emotion which had brought her so close to his son. In the carefree spirit that prevailed in Rome their youthful longing for love had awakened mutual understanding and sympathy without penetrating into their innermost being. Jenny can understand the truth of what Gert says, but this makes it no easier for her to hear his words.

Gert Gram is a gentle and noble-minded man of middle age who is attracted to Jenny because, like her, he too has had his youthful dreams of happiness. In his early years he had been an artist and designer, but with his limited talent he had produced nothing more than a few skillful imitations. Despite failures and disappointment in career and marriage he has not lost hope completely. He believes that no life can be meaningless as long as one has the capacity to love someone in whom he can place his entire trust. In Jenny he sees the reflection of his own youth and ambitions and he loves her because she is an artist of genuine power and represents the image of what he once hoped to become. Jenny is first drawn to Gert out of a feeling of pity for one who has been downtrodden and has suffered much, but she then recognizes his great fortitude of soul and his willingness to help a person like herself who is bewildered and sick with longing. She, who has always been able to give help and counsel to others, is now herself in need of such help. With her restless heart she seeks warmth where she can find it and yields to Gert in the hope of discovering a more harmonious experience in his love.

However, even as she yields to Gert, Jenny realizes that her love is one born of despair. She feels humiliated that she has accepted an affection to which she cannot respond. "She was so miserably poor herself and had complained of her need to him who, she thought, was just as poor as she, and he had shown her that he was rich, gladly offering her a little kindness out of his abundance." [3]

Jenny cannot do without Gert; so she gives him the little love she has to offer, but without being inwardly committed. "He spoke of love, but her love was not what he thought it was, and she could not explain it in words. She just clung to him—and it was no grace or princely gift.—It was just a poor little begging love. She did not want him to thank her for it; she merely wanted him to be fond of her and say nothing." [4]

Jenny knows that the liaison with Gert can be only temporary and for that reason finds it all the more humiliating and degrading to think that she has accepted his love when it was merely shelter which she sought in his arms and because she did not have the strength to reject the one person who loved her. "She had had to speak words stronger and more passionate than her feelings, and he had believed these words. And it happened again and again. When she came to him depressed, discouraged and tired of thinking of how it would all end, and saw that he understood—then she spoke again the tender words, feigning more feeling than she had, and he believed her." [5]

Jenny broods continually because the affair with Gert is only a surrogate for the true love which she has always craved. She has never sought a lover or an adventure but a master whose true love might have enriched her life to such an extent that she would have desired nothing else in the world. Mixed with this poignant longing is a bitter feeling of repentance for having done such a great wrong to the man whose child she now carries.

When the relationship becomes unendurable to Jenny she decides to return to her painting, although she doubts that this can be of much help to her now. She leaves Oslo and travels to Copenhagen and from there to a small fishing village near Warnemünde in northern Germany where she gives birth to her child.

The death of the child within a few weeks is a terrible blow from which Jenny is unable to recover. After a long and painful illness she returns to Rome hoping to find there in familiar surroundings the inspiration and courage to begin work again.

Gunnar Heggen, an artist friend of her youth, meets her in Rome and tries to stir up her flagging spirits with words of encouragement, but Jenny feels that there is nothing in life which can have any further meaning for her. She has been the master of her own fate and holds no one responsible for her sad lot.

"One day," she said slowly, "I changed my course for a moment. I found it so difficult and hard to live the life I considered the most worthy—so lonely, you see. I turned off the road for a moment—I wanted to be young and to play. And so I came out into a current that carried me away—ending in something I never for a second had thought possible. . . .

"But what goal did I have anyway?" she said with a sudden vehemence. "I wanted to live in such a way that I need never be ashamed of myself either as a woman or as an artist. Never to do a thing I did not think right. I wanted to be upright, firm, and good, and have no one else's sorrow on my conscience—. And what was the origin of the wrong—the cause of it all . . . ? Was it that I yearned for love without having any particular man whose love I wanted? Was that so strange? Or was it so strange that I wanted to believe that Helge when he came, was the one I had been longing for?—until at last I really believed it myself? That was the beginning and everything else resulted from that—. I believed that I could make them happy, Gunnar,—and yet I did only harm—." [6]

Gunnar has always loved Jenny and of all people he alone understands the reason for her suffering and longing. He too has learned that life is meaningless and hearts empty if there is no more than work to depend on, and that the greatest joys exist only when they can be shared with someone else. It is therefore out of true love and not out of pity that he asks Jenny to marry him, but she feels that would be taxing their friendship too heavily. Having lost all faith in herself she is no longer capable of a complete love. She says to Gunnar:

You say you love me,—but I know that what you think you love in me is destroyed and dead.—It is the same old story—you are in love with some quality you dream that I possess—perhaps something that I had before or might have acquired—. But one day you would see me —as I really am—and I should only have made you unhappy too—.[7]

Jenny cannot accept Gunnar's love because in her own estimation she has fallen so low that she will never be able to rise again. She cannot restore that which has been destroyed within her and therefore takes her own life in a final moment of despair.

There is much of the melodramatic in this novel of Jenny's downfall. From a psychological standpoint it is difficult to understand the relationship between Jenny and Gert Gram, the father of her child, and it is depressing to follow in all detail each stage of her physical and moral decay. Nevertheless, Jenny's struggle to free herself from her isolation is a powerful tale, rich in wise and delicate perceptions, and the tragic end is inevitable and consistent with Jenny's high moral idealism.

In the winter of 1911 *Jenny* was the most widely read book in Norway and a favorite topic of discussion in feminist circles, where it stirred up a veritable storm of protest. It was criticized because of the frank treatment of a woman's erotic life and the many bold and realistic descriptions in certain sections of the book. However, the feminists of the time objected chiefly to the fact that Jenny is portrayed as a woman who is enslaved by her sexual nature and can find nothing of satisfying and enduring value in her work as an artist. It is true that Jenny wishes to love and be loved in all truth and dignity, but in this very longing to love another person she is attempting to break free from a condition of slavery in which a woman is merely the object of a man's love. Early in the novel she expresses her view that a woman must assert herself as an individual with a right to happiness. She says: "If any irreparable harm happens to you it is always your own fault, and if you cannot train your will to master your moods and impulses and so on—and do not have complete control of yourself, you would do best to commit suicide right away." [8]

Sigrid Undset was not a militant feminist, but neither was she an anti-feminist. She believed that every woman should be free to practice an art or a profession or occupy herself in any form of work without losing the right to love and to establish a family. In her essay "Nogen kvindesaksbetragtninger" ("Some Observations on the Suffragette Movement") she writes, "The loneliest and most worn-out worker at a typewriter, in office, shop or factory, or at a sewing machine—has the right to hope and wait and dream of a happiness as a lover and wife and mother." [9] The role of the woman as a wife and a mother and the importance of the family institution in the cultural life of a people are themes which were to recur again and again in Sigrid Undset's later works.

II   Poor Fortunes

After Sigrid Undset and Anders Svarstad were married in the spring of 1912, they went to London where they lived in Hammersmith until December of that year. This was a happy interlude in Sigrid Undset's life, for during these months she was free to attend the theater, visit museums, absorb herself in the reading of English Renaissance literature and also enjoy the beauty of the English countryside. With the exception of Rome there was no city she found more exciting than London. It was difficult for her to realize that she was now a happily married woman. To her friend Nini Roll Anker she wrote: "I shall never feel like a properly married woman, even though people address me as 'Madame'. It seems to me that I belong to that group of lonely unmarried women who have never known what happiness is, unless they perchance find it in some irregular or secret love." [10] In a collection of short stories, *Fattige skjebner* (*Poor Fortunes*), written while she was living in London, Sigrid Undset reveals her sensitive understanding for the plight of such hapless, ordinary people and reaffirms her belief in the sacred right of every individual to live his life in all human dignity.

Although these stories have less of an autobiographical nature than her earlier works, they are nevertheless written with the same intensity of feeling. The characters, drawn from the middle-class society of Oslo at the turn of the century, are depicted in realistic fashion and with a humor and gentle satire worthy of Dickens or Chekhov. Sigrid Undset has great respect for the noble qualities of these simple people, but she has also learned through experience that because of loneliness and frustration men and women are sometimes forced to act in a manner unworthy of their better selves, as victims of their own foibles and weaknesses.

Selma Bröter is one of several office employees in their mid-thirties who have experienced no love in the dreary atmosphere of various rented rooms and boardinghouses. In direct contrast to

Selma, withering away in unfulfillment, is Beate Nordahl, young, vibrant, and pulsating with life, who leaves her office post to marry the young architect Stener Gundersen. Selma is basically a kind and loyal soul, but she is not entirely without envy of Beate's happiness in marriage and motherhood. Lonely and frustrated as she is, she creates her own imaginary world of admirers. Her erotic experience is limited to an occasional obscene remark directed to her by some vulgar person on the street. There is keen satire in Sigrid Undset's description of the ridicule to which these aging spinsters are subjected. However, Selma shows her true worth when her widowed sister comes to her with her child in need of help. It is Selma who assumes the responsibility for their care, just as she has always sacrificed herself in the past for the welfare of her family. Selma is a pathetic figure, but Beate, the only one who has any feeling of compassion for her, is content to think that in the vicarious pleasure of caring for her sister's child Selma has found the greatest happiness she has ever known.

Miss Smith-Tellefsen, like Selma Bröter a middle-aged spinster, is the housekeeper for a widower and his three young children. She is an efficient worker in the care of home and children and with the passing of time has come to entertain hopes of marriage to her employer. However, although he respects her and appreciates all she has done for his motherless children, he is annoyed by her constant chatter and the unctious concern with which she constantly hovers about him. When he marries a distant cousin, Miss Smith-Tellefsen has to leave his home and find employment elsewhere. In her new position she is forced to hear words of abuse and indignity from her employer. Humiliated without any just reason, she is a forlorn picture of despair and dejection as she breaks down in tears.

The best short story of this collection is *Simonsen,* a tale of an elderly man of almost sixty years who has never been able to make much of his life. At home he was subjected to nagging and criticism as long as his wife was alive and at work he suffered rebukes and insults. He could never keep a job for any length of time because of his general inefficiency and weakness for drink. After his wife's death, he met Olga, a poor seamstress, and with her a good measure of contentment and happiness had come into his life. Simonsen lives with Olga and their six-year-old illegitimate daughter Svanhild. He has often thought of marrying Olga

but has always been afraid of incurring the displeasure of his son
Sigurd and his proud daughter-in-law, for it is only through Sigurd's business connections that he has ever been able to find any
work at all.

Just before Christmas Simonsen has again been dismissed from
his job and has to appeal once more to his son for help. Sigurd
and his wife hope to make an end of Simonsen's liaison with the
seamstress by offering him a position in the small provincial town
where they live. They make it very clear that it will be impossible
for Olga to join him, for there would be no opportunity for her to
open a dressmaking shop in such a small town. Much as Olga
loves Simonsen she realizes that they are in no position to oppose
the wishes of Sigurd and his wife. As poor people they have no
alternative; Simonsen must accept this offer of help. Although he
knows he must leave his little family, Simonsen spends Christmas
Eve with Olga and Svanhild instead of returning immediately
with Sigurd and his daughter-in-law to their home. He dreams of
the time when Olga and Svanhild will be able to join him, since
only with them does he feel the warmth of true love and devotion.
However, Olga knows that this time will never come, for there is
someone greater than ourselves who rules over us and determines
the course of our lives.

On Christmas day Simonsen makes the bitter choice between
love and economic necessity; with tears in his eyes he leaves Olga
and his daughter and returns to his son. Of *Simonsen* Professor A.
H. Winsnes writes: "There is satire of the tenderest kind, where it
trembles on the verge between tears and laughter, as in the mas-
terly short story *Simonsen,* where the dissonances of life are resolved in a humour closely related to that of Dickens." [11]

The other stories in *Poor Fortunes* reveal the same universal
pathos and sympathy which Sigrid Undset felt for the poor of all
age groups. One of these stories, *Förste möte* (*First Meeting*), is a
short account of a young girl's first encounter with poverty and
the lasting impact which it has on her in later life. The sketch has
autobiographical overtones, for in *The Longest Years* Sigrid
Undset makes frequent reference to the feeling of humiliation and
shame that came over her when she learned from her mother that
they were poor.[12]

III Spring

Like *Jenny,* Sigrid Undset's next novel *Vaaren* (*Spring*), published in 1914, is also a love story, but one in which two idealistic and sensitive young people, Rose and Torkild, after a difficult period of adjustment are finally able to achieve a harmonious relationship in their marriage. Rose is proud and virtuous, and like Jenny she longs for an enduring love that will take her completely and "tear her out of herself." In *Jenny* the question of marriage is discussed in its relationship to the artist's personal life and his creative work, but never within the framework of any social context. *Spring,* on the other hand, is a social novel, in which all characters are viewed in the light of the homes from which they come and the obligations which they take upon themselves in establishing their own homes. Torkild and Rose, who have been friends since childhood, come from different types of homes. Torkild, together with his brother Aksel and his sister Doris, comes from a broken home. Aksel says of his parents: "They lived their own feverish lives so intensely, that they had little time to think of their children. Wherever his father and mother lived together in the same house, one could never speak of a home." [13] The parents finally separate and the mother, a drug addict, takes her own life.

The home of Mrs. Wegner, Rose's widowed mother, on the other hand, is for Torkild a delightful world of enchantment where he spends many hours in a relaxed atmosphere so lacking in his own home. His older brother Aksel, at one time Torkild's rival for Rose's affection, says to her: "Every little thing about you is a reminder of the home you came from. Wherever you were to go, that would become home, and the man you were to love would have his home in you." [14]

In the figure of the Danish-born Mrs. Wegner, whose very presence radiates warmth and affection, Sigrid Undset has drawn a picture of her own mother. From earliest childhood Torkild has loved Mrs. Wegner as his own mother and gradually he transfers this love to her young daughter. As long as he has known Rose she has possessed everything he has always so hopelessly longed for. "And now he came to long for her. In that moment when he could take her in his arms, he would embrace everything that he had ever longed for in embitterment and despondency through all the long years of his hopelessness and despair and shame." [15]

However, Torkild is unable to awaken any responsive love in
the young girl, who looks upon him merely as a brother or as a
dear friend whom she has known all her life. Like Jenny she too
has her dreams of happiness, but Torkild plays no part in these
dreams. She tells him that she wishes to love someone who can
change her completely. She says: "I always believe that one day I
shall meet someone and then everything in me will say: 'Go to
him, do everything he wishes—you are his, just like a ring on his
finger. He can take you and carry you or put you down, but you
are his.'" [16] Torkild understands that there is more than a little
narcissistic self-love in Rose's mental image of the man she hopes
to love and in the friendly kiss she once gave him. He says: "It
was for her own sake that she had kissed him. It was herself she
was in love with, now and then and always—herself or the ideal
picture she constructed of herself and wished to resemble at any
price." [17]

After her mother's death Rose leaves home to take an office job,
but like most of Sigrid Undset's working girls she detests her work
and is unable to find friends in office or boardinghouse. She returns to Torkild, not because her feelings toward him are greatly
changed, but because she is unable to bear the burden of her loneliness. She thinks to herself: "She had accepted his love as a matter of course, as something which belonged to her without end,
but she had never tried to assess what it meant for her. Now she
knew. It was not Torkild she longed for, but she knew that she
could never shut him out of her heart without leaving a sore spot
behind. And she knew that she could not do without his love
either." [18]

Torkild and Rose are married, but within a few months difficulties arise for the young couple. They have no friends or interests
beside themselves. In marriage Rose finds no deep-felt experience,
for although she wishes to be loved and caressed, she does not
respond completely to Torkild's love. When her child is still-born,
the only bond between husband and wife seems to be broken.
Unpleasant scenes lead to long periods of silence. Torkild believes
it was only through a series of accidental circumstances that Rose
was drawn to him and in marrying her he merely took unfair advantage of her loneliness. For this reason he does not wish to have
any children, for he could never look upon them without thinking

that they had been brought into the world not because of Rose's love for him, but because it would be the only way he could bind her to himself.

Torkild and Rose separate again, this time to avoid bitterness and recriminations, but they are later reconciled through the intercession of Betsy, a mutual friend. They can now finally look forward to a harmonious married life with a clear concept of what each partner may expect of the other in their new relationship.

At first glance the account of the struggles which these young people must go through may seem too finespun, and the self-analysis to which they subject themselves too subtle. However, Rose and Torkild are both honest and straightforward young people who act with integrity and in accordance with their natures. Both must make adjustments before they fully mature. Through Torkild's love Rose has been transformed from a self-centered young girl to a better, more capable and affectionate woman, and the experience has likewise made Torkild a more tolerant and understanding human being. The sense of responsibility toward family and society which he develops in spite of his unfortunate family background is a theme which Sigrid Undset touches upon repeatedly in her later works. At one time his sister Doris, speaking of their father, remarks: "I loved father, because he had the courage to live his own life after his own fashion, without concern for others. It is an individual's most sacred right to live his own life." To this Torkild answers: "No, no man has the right to do that, for no man can live his own life without reaching out into the lives of others." [19]

Rose is even more conscious of the important role which the family plays in human society. She has come from a home in which the bonds of loyalty were very closely knit. Indeed, she has been surrounded and protected with so much love and affection that she has been denied the right to assume any responsibilities. As a result she has become withdrawn and unresponsive to the needs of others. When she is left alone after the death of her mother, she is unable or unwilling to adjust herself to the new circumstances and thus returns to Torkild, her only friend. She knows that she has been egoistic, but she also knows that all would have been different in their marriage if her child had lived, for it is Rose's calling in life to be a mother. She tells Torkild: "I was not created to be married without children. You should know me well enough for that. I should have a whole flock of young ones about me." [20]

Betsy, the friend who has brought about the reconciliation, has already found happiness in her young children. She is of a more robust and uncomplicated nature than Rose and therefore speaks in a frank and realistic manner. "You two are so odd," she says. "Somehow you make life so complicated and strange and romantic." [21] For Sigrid Undset marriage has no perpetual romantic enchantment. It is, however, a binding arrangement, whether it turns out to be completely satisfying or not. In her article "Some Observations on the Suffragette Movement," written while she was living in England, she states that the demands of enfranchised women for self-sufficiency can very easily be misunderstood, for they tend to reduce the significance of woman's all-important role as a wife and mother. She adds: "Even if being a mother means in itself no more than a physical fact—this physical fact means that in human society a woman can become nothing better than a good mother, and nothing much worse than a bad one." [22]

For Sigrid Undset the family is the nucleus of civilization, and within the family it is the wife and mother who in the dignity of her position preserves this rich heritage. The feminists believe that they can win freedom by breaking away from the family and demanding equal rights in a newly industrialized and highly competitive society. Actually it is the mother in the household with her instinct for social solidarity who possesses a greater measure of freedom. By accepting the responsibility for the physical and spiritual welfare of the family she is able to maintain sovereign power in precisely that area where she has always exercised the greatest influence and enjoyed the greatest respect, that is, in her role as wife and mother.

Like Betsy, Rose too finds joy and happiness in her family. She adopts the orphaned nephew of Torkild, and Sigrid Undset would have us understand that she and Torkild will also have children of their own. In contrast to Betsy and Rose, Sigrid Undset also introduces a representative of enfranchised women in the person of Mary Lied, a neighbor of Rose and Torkild. Mary Lied looks upon marriage as an outmoded institution, but a necessary evil until the time comes when society is so organized that it can take over the responsibility for the care of children. She believes that society or the state should make payment to a mother who wishes to take care of her own children. However, if the mother considers herself incapable of doing so, or if she believes she has talents and abilities which should be channeled into other directions, then the children should be placed in institutions where they may be cared for by specially trained women. Mary Lied leaves her husband and children to live with a man whose work and interests are more to her liking. Ironically, however, she is soon rejected by her lover and forced to return to her home and acknowledge the error of her ways and of her thinking.

In 1919 Sigrid Undset wrote an article "Begrepsforvirring" ("Confusion of Ideas")[23] in answer to Katti Anker Möller's pamphlet "Kvindernes fødselspolitik" ("A Birth Policy for Women"). Mrs. Möller recommends that the state make cash payments for children handed over to it by mothers. She speaks of strikes, wage disputes, women as "birth machines" and children as "goods." Sigrid Undset does not take any of this seriously, but she deplores the fact that such a materialistic attitude can exist at all, for she considers it a threat to the dignity of human life. She gives a further answer to Mrs. Möller in her article "Efterskrift" ("Postscript") in which she quotes a motto taken from a ballad:

> How on earth can the green grass grow,
> When a son can't find his mother true?[24]

IV Images in a Mirror

In 1917, while living in the East Aker section of Oslo Sigrid Undset wrote two short stories, *Fru Hjelde* (*Mrs. Hjelde*) and *Fru Waage* (*Mrs. Waage*), both of which appeared in the volume *Splinten av troldspeilet* (only *Mrs. Hjelde* appears in the English translation entitled *Images in a Mirror*). These stories are closely related in theme to the novel *Spring,* in that they are concerned with the difficulties young people encounter in marriage and the adjustments they are forced to make if their married life is to have any meaning. However, *Spring* is written from the standpoint of both husband and wife, who must share equally in the responsibilities imposed upon them in marriage, whereas *Images in a Mirror* is written from the woman's point of view with the light focused directly on the figures of Uni Hjelde and Harriet Waage.

Mrs. Hjelde is a sequel to *The Happy Age*. Uni, now married to Kristian Hjelde and expecting her fourth child, lives in genteel poverty on a bleak and dreary street in the western part of Oslo. She has long since given up her theatrical career in order to be a devoted wife and mother, but she continues to feel an inner conflict between her desire for self-expression as an actress and the necessity of withdrawing from a life filled with brilliance and excitement to accept the virtual serfdom of a middle-class wife. Kristian, an unimaginative but industrious husband, is so preoccupied with the task of making ends meet, that he does not have the vision to see how much Uni suffers from the drudgery and physical strain of caring for her home and children. Even though the family is the one reality in Uni's life, her thoughts continuously carry her back to her youth when life was still an unwritten book and she could dream of the happiness which lay before her. She loves Kristian, but some part of her nature has been unfulfilled, so that she has never known complete happiness. She tells Kristian: "I want to feel life like a taste in my mouth. I want to know that there is a happiness which fills and satisfies a human being—at least once in my life." [25]

Uni finds some excitement in the attention given to her by Vegard, an old acquaintance whom she has not seen for many years. For her the opportunity of talking with someone is in itself a welcome relief from the tedium of her daily routine, and in addition she is flattered to think that Vegard can still find her attractive and charming. Actually she is not interested in him, but even if she were, nothing would have come of this flirtation, for Uni could never be unfaithful to her husband. Kristian is the only man she has ever loved, and absolute loyalty is her response to the unquestioning faith he has in her.

The experience seems to bring Uni and Kristian together again, for it breaks down the wall of silence that has separated them for such a long time. Calmly and dispassionately they speak out the longing they have always felt for each other, and they ask themselves what life can hold in store for them. Uni wonders why she should use up her youth and wear herself out in raising a flock of children who in turn will wear themselves out in the same way for their children as they search for something that doesn't exist. Kristian answers that he too has thought about this and all that he can say is that it *is* so. Everyone works to give his children a better chance, and those who have no children work for the future, that is, for other people's children, "for they all know that happiness is something too great to be contained within the compass of a single human life." [26]

From Kristian Uni learns that one must choose between repudiation of responsibility on the one hand and fulfillment of duty and obedience on the other. By removing the splinter of the magic mirror from her eye she can view life and its purpose from a new perspective and she can see the danger of clinging too long to a self-portrait she has drawn of herself. She chooses duty as she remarks: "I am just an ordinary average human being and I can no more run away from my place than a soldier can desert his post in battle. It is better to believe that one is there of one's own free will than because one is forced to be there." [27]

Uni has made some sacrifice, but she has gained the knowledge that life demands a limitation of personality rather than its free development. Holding her youngest child in her lap she muses:

How could I at my age believe in happiness—or doubt it?

Such happiness as Kristian and I had together once is like a shooting star, and when we see a star fall we should remember to wish our dearest wish. In the fleeting moments when caresses are new and wonderful we should understand and order our lives. But I wonder how many know how to do it.

And our happiness in the children is so much a matter of course that we don't think about it. All the times when our hearts seem to glitter with joy—at the comical things they say, and their first funny attempts at walking, and when they begin to show human sense and want to love us, and when we touch them, or when we get over a fright, or when a threatened illness turns out not so bad as we thought. We never think that all these tiny little gleams are what make for happiness. Yet these are the things we live from. No human being could go on living without some happiness, but we never think of it while we have it. It is only when we are miserable that we become conscious of ourselves. So long as I have the children I can live—cheerfully, no matter what happens.

And when I think that after all Kristian and I have loved each other, and still love each other in a way, and as things are between us now, so they will continue to be as long as we both live—then I think I can meet death too when it comes.[28]

The story of Uni Hjelde is told in a straightforward way without the least touch of sentimentality. In the hands of a less gifted writer it might have become a banal and shallow tale, but Sigrid Undset follows the course of Uni's shifting emotions with wisdom and understanding. In the end Uni suppresses all personal vanity and accepts the responsibility which she owes to her family. In a letter to Nini Roll Anker, Sigrid Undset states that this sense of responsibility to the home must be equally great for all women, including those involved in creative work, which makes special demands on their time and energy. She writes: "I have never believed in 'sacred egotism,' neither for artists nor for anyone else. Individualism, if by that we mean the right to demand special privileges for one's own individuality at the expense of others, merely makes it easier for power mentalities to subjugate others." [29]

In Harriet Waage, a contrasting figure to Uni Hjelde, there is much that reminds the reader of Marta Oulie. Harriet's father was a freethinker who sought the law of life in his own small consciousness. For him as for many "progressive" people at the end of the nineteenth century, there were no longer any standards of spiritual value, because God and the sanctity of religion had been eliminated from their lives as something old-fashioned. Without any spiritual anchorage, they allowed themselves to be driven on by impulse or the tractable "law of nature," with the result that their actions had relevance to nothing beyond that which served their self-interest.

Harriet Waage is such a self-indulgent individual, married off while still very young to a wealthy cousin, Fredrik Waage. There is no happiness in this marriage, for both Fredrik and Harriet live their own circumscribed lives and neither has the warmth of heart to be concerned with the needs and interests of the other. When their young son is drowned, Harriet receives less sympathy and consolation from her husband than from a friend, Henning Damm. She soon leaves her husband to become Henning's mistress, and later his wife. Henning is a married man with two children, but Harriet is insensitive to the fact that she is ruining two homes. She knows only that her life continues to be empty and that her new marriage will bring her no more happiness than the old one. Like Marta Oulie she has sought only what could afford her pleasure and gratification without demanding any personal sacrifice on her part. Her life is disordered because it has never been related to any set of moral values.

Alice Falch, Harriet's cousin, tries to explain to her that things might be better if one believed in God and understood everything in relation to Him and not primarily in relation to oneself. She thinks that people of their generation can never be really happy, because they have erected themselves as an absolute in place of God and seek the cause of their fate in their lonely little egos. In olden days people likewise often listened to the counsels of the devil, the world, or their own flesh. However, even as they did so, they knew they were committing sins against God and they never failed to remember that they were part of God's supernatural kingdom. Alice thinks that it must have been better to atone for a few precious moments of happiness through a lifetime of penance and prayer than to live on and become bored and coarse and common as people do nowadays.

Sigrid Undset's early works are all characterized by a severe ethical idealism, but here for the first time there is an indication that she has found a religious faith which has its metaphysical basis in a supernatural world of the spirit.

V   The Wise Virgins

The title of Sigrid Undset's next collection of three short stories, *De kloge jomfruer* (*The Wise Virgins*), which appeared in 1918, suggests a further development in her religious thinking. However, once again, just as in *Mrs. Hjelde* and *Poor Fortunes*, the basic theme in two of the three stories is the longing of ordinary average women of the working class for husband, home, and children. With moral heroism these fine women meet disappointment in marriage, but find a rare glow of life in the love they can offer their children.

Perhaps the most moving of this collection is *Thjodolf*, a tale of a childless middle-aged woman, Helene Johansen, who becomes the foster-mother of a six-weeks-old child rejected by its real mother, a delinquent slattern. For Helene life has been empty since she had lost her own child ten years earlier. Her husband, Julius, is lighthearted and irresponsible and seeks his friends and relaxation outside the home. The infant Thjodolf thus fills a vacant spot in Helene's heart, and she gives the child all her motherly love.

After some time the real mother, Fanny Erdahl, returns to lay claim to her child. As Helene and Julius have not legally adopted Thjodolf, they must cede to the mother's wish and return the child to her. However, the child is so sadly neglected by its real mother that it soon becomes seriously ill, and Fanny begs Helene to take the child back into her care. Thjodolf is thus shuttled back to Helene, who does her utmost to restore the child to health. She is able to win back the love and affection of the child, but not its health. For one whole night before he dies Thjodolf rests in Helene's arms. In the morning she notices the black and blue marks on her arms where Thjodolf had clung to her in his last struggle. At the child's funeral Helene suffers a further shock, when she learns that Julius has become involved in an affair with Fanny.

For Helene the love she can give Thjodolf is the very essence of her life. She is just an ordinary woman with no special gifts or talents, and in contrast to the wayward Fanny Erdahl she lacks a certain spark which can kindle excitement in men's minds. However, she is loyal and steadfast, and her greatness lies in her devotion to home and family as the one living reality in all existence.

Gunnvald og Emma (*Gunnvald and Emma*) is another tale of a fine woman from the same ordinary background as Helene Johansen. Emma, the owner of a small dairy shop, becomes the second wife of Gunnvald and the stepmother of his four children. Earlier Gunnvald, a nineteen-year-old youth, had married the factory worker Klara, who was four or five years older than he and already a woman with a sordid past. "Some women feel their sex," writes Sigrid Undset, "as an impulse to live for someone else, but Klara was one of those who feel it as something which gives them the right to live on someone else." [30]

Even after their marriage Klara continued to live a dissolute life, but nevertheless Gunnvald loved her intensely, for she was to him the only ray of sunshine in an otherwise drab existence. During her final illness he cared for her like a faithful servant and after her death he looked forward to the time when he would be rejoined with her in heaven.

Emma, however, is a woman of noble character. When Gunnvald marries her, he wins a woman who gives him her true love and concerns herself with the care and well-being of his children as though they were her own. She makes a special effort to help Mathilde, the oldest of her stepchildren, who gives every indication of developing into the same type of woman her mother had been. However, Emma has little rapport with the children, whose minds have already been shaped and influenced by the climate of permissiveness which earlier had prevailed in their home. Worst of all, Emma is unable to win the affection of Gunnvald whose memories of Klara's passionate love make him insensitive to the excellent qualities of his second wife. The only happiness Emma knows is the opportunity to care for her little family and to give it all the warmth of her unselfish love. At one time she is close to despair when she learns that this love is not returned. With the birth of her own child, however, a new dimension is added to her life. Gunnvald is finally drawn close to her, for now for the first time he begins to appreciate Emma's true worth.

Smaapiker (*Little Girls*) is a delightful sketch about two twelve-year-old girls, Sif and Elna, who used to be close friends before Elna moved away to live in another section of Oslo. Now Elna returns to pay an infrequent visit to her friend, and the two girls look forward to spending a wonderful day together in Oslo's beautiful environs. On their promenade they come upon a two-year-old boy who has wandered away from his nursemaid. The two girls vie for the affection of the little fellow, making use of all the feminine wiles at their command much in the manner of adults competing for some greater prize. Jealousy rears its ugly head as soon as the young lad seems to prefer one girl to the other. The nursemaid comes to retrieve the child, and the girls return home in silence. After a brief farewell in front of Sif's home they part never to see one another again.

With the publication of *The Wise Virgins* in 1918 Sigrid Undset brought to a close the first period of her literary career. Her novels of contemporary life written between 1907 and 1918 belong in the mainstream of Norwegian realistic writing, which may be said to have begun in 1871. In that year Georg Brandes, the great Danish literary critic, in a series of lectures given at the University of Copenhagen, propounded the thesis that literature should show its vitality by "submitting problems to debate." With this dictum he passed final judgment on the entire movement of National Romanticism and prepared the way for a realistic literature that concerned itself with the agitations of contemporary life.

Sigrid Undset did not become involved in political or religious

controversy, nor was she interested in defending any literary doctrine. It was her purpose merely to reproduce without any embel-
lishment a cross-section of that life which she knew so well and in
which ordinary people of a lower middle-class background were
the protagonists. Her first novels thus represent a continuation of
a long uninterrupted realistic tradition in modern Norwegian literature. Like other women authors in nineteenth- and twentieth-
century Norway, such as Camilla Collett, Amalie Skram, Nini Roll
Anker, and Barbra Ring, Sigrid Undset too draws a gloomy and
somber picture of contemporary society. There is a certain regu-
larity and even monotony in the humble outward circumstances
of the characters appearing in her early novels, but their inner
conflicts are no less intense for that reason. Sigrid Undset has
drawn her material from personal experience. As a woman of
great moral strength, she recognized and admired the loyalty and
courage of some men and women, but she was also realist enough
to know that frailty, shallowness, and moral indifference are likewise part of all human experience.

It is at this point that Sigrid Undset adds a new dimension to
her writing. She can understand the plight of unfortunate
wretches who are victims of their own weaknesses. She can even
sympathize with them, but with her stern moral idealism she cannot pardon or forgive any fault. Other writers of the time would
have blamed extenuating circumstances or society itself for the
individual's misfortune, but Sigrid Undset states fearlessly and
unequivocally that each man is responsible for his own fate. He
must seek his happiness not within his own narrow soul, but in the
acceptance of his obligations to others. He cannot evade the hard
laws he has imposed on himself, for then life would not be human
life. This sense of responsibility finds its highest expression within
the framework of home and family and in the relations between
men and women or between parents and children. Later her
Christian faith was to broaden this concept of loyalty and
responsibility even further, so that she could look upon all human
behavior in relationship not only to the commonplace but also to
the supernatural world of the spirit.

CHAPTER 4

The Middle Ages

ALTHOUGH she first became known to the Norwegian reading public through her novels of contemporary life, Sigrid Undset's greatest claim to literary renown came with the publication of her two novels of medieval life, *Kristin Lavransdatter* and *Olav Audunssön*, written between 1920 and 1927. The author's interest in medieval Norway was, as we have seen, originally kindled by her father Ingvald Undset, an archeologist of international reputation. In the autobiographical account of her childhood reminiscences, *The Longest Years*, the author tells of the small group of her father's friends and colleagues, among them the distinguished philologist Sophus Bugge, who used to meet at the Undset home to discuss literary, historical, and archeological topics ranging from the Eddic poems to the runic alphabet of the Black Sea region.

After her father's death in 1893, she continued her historical studies, and as early as 1902 was occupied with the writing of a historical novel which had its setting in the middle of the thirteenth century. The novel, however, was rejected by the Gyldendal Publishing Company in Copenhagen, and Sigrid Undset apparently destroyed the manuscript some twenty years later when the first volume of *Olav Audunssön* was published.

In 1909 she published *Fortellingen om Viga-Ljot og Vigdis*, a tenth-century tale, in which both style and content are strongly influenced by the Icelandic sagas and the heathen revenge ethic of that early family society.

In her studies Sigrid Undset was able to make use of all the material on Norway's medieval history that scholars of the late nineteenth and early twentieth century had already assembled. As a result, her historical fiction is characterized by a solidity of knowledge which is in sharp contrast to the reconstructed history and pageantry of Sir Walter Scott's novels written in the early decades of the nineteenth century when such source material was not yet available. As a historian Sigrid Undset went directly to her primary sources. She acknowledges her debt to scholars in the field of medieval Norse studies, such as Finnur Jónsson, Sigurður Nordal, and Magnus Olsen, but it was her friend Professor Fredrik Paasche who was of the greatest help to her in her research. It was he who called her attention to the *Diplomatarium Norvegicum*, that rich storehouse of laws, documents, and letters, which throws so much light on the political, social, and religious conditions of medieval Norway.

Sigrid Undset's scholarship, however, at no time weighs heavily on the reader. The great wealth of cultural-historical material is skillfully blended with the action of her novels so as to produce works of great artistic effect. Actually, she is not interested in re-creating history. In each of her two medieval novels she has deliberately selected a period of Norwegian history for which there are only few historical records. In this way she can give free rein to her fantasy and imagination, and by creating an illusion of reality she can devote her entire attention to the inner lives of her characters. Sigrid Undset never cared to draw any sharp line between past and present. In the past people were guided by their intellect in making the proper choice between good and evil just as they are today. Manners and customs may change, but the human heart remains the same through the ages. It is her fine insight into this human heart and her ability to judge people in relation to the social, political, and religious circumstances peculiar to their own times which enable her to present such a galaxy of figures in all clarity and convincing psychological realism.

Sigrid Undset's modern novels are realistic portrayals of middle-class life in Oslo as she had occasion to observe it at first hand. The characters she describes within the limited confines of their milieu reflect the morality of their age. Many of them are modern pagans who seek happiness within the narrow circle of their own heart, but have no sense of responsibility toward others. Egoistic individualism demands its rights, but does not concern itself with its obligations. In the Middle Ages, on the other hand, Sigrid Undset recognized the existence of a society with great vitality despite the many conflicting interests of temporal and spiritual powers. Men and women of that time were stirred by the same emotions as they are today. They could be cruel and ruthless and

they were driven by the same instincts and passions which domi-
nate the minds of men today, six or seven hundred years later.
However, they knew nothing of the egocentric personality cult
which began with the Renaissance. Sigrid Undset's medieval
characters are clearly defined personalities, but they are not indi-
vidualists in the modern sense. They recognized themselves as
members of a family and they gave consideration for the welfare
and honor of this family priority over their personal happiness.
Furthermore, through Christianity the fundamental solidarity of
all mankind was revealed. All men, slaves as well as masters, were
children of God, created in His image and called to be His servants. All life had an eternal perspective and man, having his origin
in God, was part of a supernatural kingdom. Tensions were often
developed, however, when man set his self-will against the will of
God. In the dualistic battle between the forces of good and evil he
might rise in defiance of God or succumb to the temptations of the
devil, but he was then well aware of his sin, for there was never
any doubt in his mind that God was the center of all creation, the
one and only reality. Eugenia Kielland has therefore very appro-
priately used the words of St. Augustine as a motto for her essay
on Sigrid Undset: *Fecisti nos ad te et inquietum est cor nostrum
donec requiescat in te* (*Thou hast made us for Thyself, O Lord,
and our hearts know no rest until they rest in Thee*).[1]

I   Kristin Lavransdatter

It is against the backdrop of events of the first half of the fourteenth century that the action of *Kransen* (*The Bridal Wreath*),
the first part of *Kristin Lavransdatter*, takes place.[2] Kristin grows
up at Jörundgaard in Gudbrandsdal at a time when the country,
under the able rule of Haakon V, is enjoying for the most part a
period of undisturbed peace. Her father, Lavrans Björgulfssön,
originally from Skog in the Oslo region, has served in the king's
bodyguard as a youth and thus knows something of the ways of
court life. Now that peace reigns in the land, he lives quietly as a
sturdy and industrious landowner who has gained the respect of
his tenant farmers through his kindness and upright dealings. He
is pious and God-fearing, faithful in keeping the fasts and always
prepared to shelter pilgrims as they make their way up the valley
to the shrine of St. Olav in Christ Church at Nidaros (Trondheim). His wife Ragnfrid is equally pious, but more reserved

and heavy of mood. Although there is not much room for sentiment or show of feelings in this family, there are nevertheless
strong bonds of affection among all members, and particularly between Lavrans and his eldest daughter Kristin.

One morning when Kristin is seven years old, she joins her father and his men on a visit to their summer farm in the mountains.
While the men are resting, Kristin wanders off to the side of a
mountain stream, and in a pool as clear as crystal she gazes at her
reflection to learn whether it is true that she bears any likeness to
her father, as people have already observed. She sees her own
image rising from the bottom of the pool, but then she sees another figure, that of an elf-maiden, pale with waving flaxen hair.
The figure holds in her hand a wreath of golden flowers with
which she beckons to Kristin. The young girl shrieks in fright, but
when her father comes to her side she knows that she is safe.
Kristin has seen the elf-maiden who according to folk belief is
sometimes able to lure unsuspecting victims into her mountain
abode. The elf-maiden, however, signifies more than that. She is a
symbol of the beautiful but dangerous world of the senses which
makes use of all its snares and temptations to entice people who
would put their own desires and gratifications above the higher
order of a supernatural will.

On another occasion while visiting the cathedral in Hamar on
Lake Mjösa, Kristin is overwhelmed by the grandeur of the
Gothic edifice and the painted glass panels depicting Biblical
scenes in all the fairest colors.[3] Here, too, she meets for the first
time a humble Franciscan monk, Brother Edvin, who explains to
her the meaning of the beautiful pictures. In the figure of this
devout and gentle beggar monk there is much that reminds the
reader of St. Francis of Assisi who dedicated himself to poverty
and lived to minister to the needs of the sick and afflicted. This
type of medieval religiosity, characterized by its simplicity and
humility, but also by its joy in living, always made the deepest
impression on Sigrid Undset.

Kristin has had some Christian training from her parish priest
and she is able to experience a sense of reverence for the glory of
God, but she cannot as yet understand the full meaning of
Brother Edvin's words. To her remark that the dragon on the
painting with St. Christina seems too small, he answers: "Dragons
and all such that serve the devil seem great only as long as there is

fear in ourselves. However, if a man seeks God with all his heart and soul and draws his strength from Him, then the devil's power immediately suffers such swift defeat that his tools become small and powerless—dragons and evil spirits sink down and become no bigger than gnomes and cats and crows." [4] He adds: "There is no one, Kristin, who does not love and fear God, but it is because our hearts are divided between love of God and fear of the devil on the one hand and love of the world and the flesh on the other, that we are unhappy in life and death." [5]

When Kristin's younger sister Ulvhild suffers a crippling injury, Lavrans and Ragnfrid think of sending her into a cloister. Kristin is mindful of Brother Edvin's words that parents give only such children into God's service as are marred and crippled and for whom good husbands cannot be found. Kristin considers the possibility of becoming a nun herself in the hope that God might then work a miracle for Ulvhild. Brother Edvin had said that everything is possible in God's name, if only one had faith sufficiently great. This thought he had expressed to Kristin with the words: "If I had the true faith and love—I could take these old fur mittens and hang them upon that sunbeam over there." [6] However, Kristin thinks to herself: "She did not want to have such faith herself, she did not love the Lord and His Mother and the Saints so much, did not even want to love them *so* much—she loved the world and longed for the world." [7]

When Kristin is fifteen years old she is betrothed to Simon, the son of the knight Andres Gudmundsson. The marriage is arranged through agreement by Lavrans and Andres. Kristin is less than enthusiastic about the match, but raises no objections. Lady Aashild, a witch-woman who is tolerated in the parish only because of her high birth, has only scorn for the small-minded people in the Dale, and although she believes that Kristin can be happy with Simon, she adds that Kristin should be married to a man of the court who is bred in knightly ways and knows something of *curteisie*. She speaks of her sister's comely son Erlend as a fitting bridegroom.

Kristin has already learned something of the meaning of love in the tender affection which she has felt for her childhood playmate Arne Gyrdsson. She suffers a severe shock when she learns that he has been slain by Bentein, a youth who is being trained for the priesthood and who earlier had attempted to violate her. She cannot rid herself of a feeling of guilt, for this shameless deed could not have happened if she had followed her first impulse to enter the convent. She now understands the meaning of what she has already heard in church, that "she herself and all mankind had a sinful, carnal body which enmeshed the soul and ate into it with hard bonds." [8] She begs her father to send her to a convent, and Lavrans does so in the belief that a year spent with the sisters of Nonneseter in Oslo will bring peace of mind to the troubled maid before her marriage to Simon.

The nuns at Nonneseter receive Kristin kindly, and the interlude in the convent seems to have served its purpose. On Holy Rood Day the sisters receive permission to attend the fair in Oslo, and it is here that Kristin meets Erlend Nikulausson, the nephew of Lady Aashild. Kristin experiences a love such as she has never known before and the two swear vows of eternal faith.

"I will love you, Sir Erlend," said Kristin, "as long as you will—and thereafter I will love none other."
"Then," said Erlend slowly, "may God forsake me if any maid or woman comes to my arms before I make you mine in law and honor." [9]

To be sure, Kristin is betrothed to Simon, but according to canon law she cannot be wed against her will. However, if she were to break her pact with Simon in order to marry Erlend, it would place her father in a difficult position, for he would then have to be released from the agreement made with Simon's father.

To make matters worse, Erlend already has a mistress, Eline Ormsdatter, and two illegitimate children. Kristin feels confident that her father would not wish her to be unhappy and remarks to Brother Edvin: "When I was a girl at home, I could not understand how anything could win such power over the souls of men that they could forget the fear of sin. But now I know this much: If the wrongs men do through lust and anger cannot be atoned for, then heaven must be an empty place." [10]

Kristin and Erlend have little regard for any sense of decency or proper behavior, but give themselves over completely to their love without any consideration for the shame which they bring upon others through their actions. Simon learns of the illicit relationship between Erlend and Kristin when he confronts them at one of their clandestine meetings in a disreputable hostel in Oslo.

He wishes to spare Lavrans any knowledge of this shame and is willing to take upon himself the blame for the broken marriage pact. Simon thinks: "Surely it had never come into Lavrans' mind that he could be so betrayed by his own daughter. And now he himself was to bear the tidings and help to lie to *that* man—it was for this reason that his heart burned with sorrow and anger." [11] Simon grieves for Lavrans, whom he holds in great respect and honor, but there is sadness in his own heart, too, for he cannot forget Kristin and will never stop loving her.

The marriage of Kristin to Erlend is brought about with much deception and deceit. Eline, Erlend's paramour, dies by her own hand, but she is driven to the act by the threats of Kristin and Erlend, who must therefore also share in this guilt too. Lavrans is kept ignorant of the true relationship between Erlend and Kristin, so that he is completely duped when Erlend makes his formal suit for Kristin's hand. Kristin is so blinded by passion that she is prepared to defy her family and the whole world in order to win the man she loves. Even Lady Aashild notices that she is no longer concerned about the sorrow she brings upon her father and mother. Kristin says: "I have already done much that I would not have dared to do formerly, because it was a sin. But I didn't see then what sin brings with it—that one must tread others underfoot. Now I know that I can never give up Erlend—even though I should tread my own father underfoot." [12]

Nothing, however, can turn Lavrans' heart from his daughter. He comes to her in her mental anguish, takes her in his arms and tries to comfort her.

He bent her head back, looked down into his daughter's face, and then hid it again on his shoulder. "Little Kristin, are you so unhappy?"

"I think I shall die, father," she said, her face pressed to his.

She burst into tears, but she wept because she had felt in his caress and had seen in his eyes that he was now so worn out with pain that he could not hold out against her any more. She had overcome him.[13]

Kristin knows now that she has sinned not only against her father, but also against the divine order. Because her child is begotten outside the law she fears that it will be born with some mark of her sin upon it. She prays to Holy King Olav that he hold his hand over the innocent child in her womb and turn away God's wrath.

Even as she kneels through the Holy Mass that weds her to Erlend
she swears a vow that she will take her child in her arms and
wander barefoot to Christ Church in Nidaros and there lay down
her golden bridal wreath of maidenhood on St. Olav's altar.[14]

The sadness in Kristin's heart is in sharp contrast to the merri-
ment and high spirits of the many guests invited to the splendid
wedding celebration at Jörundgaard. The first book of the trilogy
therefore does not end in a triumph of love, but in a human defeat. Kristin, to be sure, has won Erlend, but in order to accom-
plish her purpose she has had to deceive her father and all her
kinsmen and to break God's divine law. She tries to find excuses
for her conduct, but in her heart she knows that she has committed a sin and that she must atone for it before she can again
find her rightful place in human society. In the intensity of Kristin's brooding one can observe the conflict of the two forces which
create such extreme tension in the human soul: the desire to do
God's will and the compulsion to follow the path of one's own
choosing.

The burden of Kristin's sin weighs heavily on Lavrans too. To
the certainty that Kristin has given herself to Erlend before their
marriage comes a further shock when he learns from his wife
Ragnfrid that he may not have been the father of her first child, a
son that died early in life. She has kept the secret in her heart
these many years, and it has left a festering wound in her inner
being from which she has suffered endless torment. Broken in
spirit as he is, Lavrans can nevertheless offer words of comfort to
his repentant wife, for he is a pious Christian who is devoted to
God and has always tried to obey His commandments. However,
he is also a realist and can accept the world as it is with all its
imperfections. It is not difficult for him to pardon others for their
weaknesses because he realizes that he too falls far short of the
Christian ideal which he has set for himself.

The second part of the novel, *Husfrue* (*The Mistress of Husaby*), tells of Kristin's arrival at Erlend's family estate at Husaby
farther to the north near the Trondheim Fjord and her able ad-
ministration of the manor there. Things have deteriorated badly,
much of Erlend's goods having gone to waste through the careless
management of Eline Ormsdatter. Through Kristin's industry and
perseverance the manor is again built up to a reasonable state of
order and prosperity. Erlend, who is proud of his descent from

King Skule, likes to talk about the ways of the manor in the ancient days when folks kept thralls and bondswomen for the household work. In her own mind Kristin constantly makes comparisons between life here at Husaby and at her father's home at Jörundgaard. She recalls how God's servants were always received in great honor there, but Erlend is no lover of priests and monks and pays homage only to those of high station. When she suggests to Erlend that he should inform his tenant farmers of the laws by which they should abide, he remarks that he is satisfied to let them till the fields as they see fit. He ridicules her father Lavrans for his strange custom of teaching the servants and young folk something of the law.

When Kristin's first child is born and Erlend fares south to bear the news to her parents, he also carries with him a message from Kristin. " 'Tell them at home,' she said slowly, 'that every hour since I left home I have longed to fall at my father's and mother's feet and beg them for forgiveness.' " [15]

From Erlend's brother, the monk Gunnulf, Kristin receives spiritual comfort. He explains that God sees her sorrow and repentance and that she must turn to the Virgin Mary, who has compassion for all who are sorrowful. When she remarks that she despairs of God's mercy because she has driven Eline to cast away her life, Gunnulf answers sternly: "Kristin, do you dare to think in your wicked pride that your sin can be so great that God's loving kindness is not greater?" [16] To the parish priest Eilif she has made confession, but for the sin she committed as an accomplice in Eline's death she must seek absolution from the Archbishop. St. Olav has saved her son through his intercession, and she must now fulfill her vow to make the pilgrimage to his shrine.

The account of Kristin's pilgrimage to the cathedral at Nidaros is most impressive. She arrives with her infant child at Feginsbrekka (Hill of Joy) and looks down upon the city bathed in the golden glow of the evening sun. From the green land below the spires of Christ Church tower into the bright summer heavens. She descends into the city, enters the churchyard and is overwhelmed by the bewildering riches of pillars and arches and windows. She sinks under the burden of her sin, for she knows only too well that she has never before known true repentance. She has merely feigned wretchedness, but her heart has always been hard with anger and evil thoughts. She wanted God to set aside the law, for she could not bear to be chastened. It was compassion she sought, not justice. Now as she kneels at the shrine of St. Olav she feels true contrition and the urgent wish to rise above her sin. She holds out the golden garland and her heart is about to break in penitence and in shame for she feels how unworthy she is of the mercy shown her. She prays to St. Olav that he may support her and that she may never again turn from God.

Before Kristin returns to Husaby she spends the night with her child at the women's hostel of the Minorites, the brethren of the now deceased Brother Edvin. During the night she awakes and sees that the moon is casting its pale light on the wall above her. She also sees a figure in the midst of the stream of moonlight, hovering between floor and roof. "It was Brother Edvin. He smiled, and his smile was unspeakably tender—a little roguishly merry, just as when he lived on earth.—Then the monk laughed and held up an old, heavy fur mitten toward her. Then he hung it on the moonbeam and left it there. Then he smiled still more, nodded to her, and melted away." [17]

During the following years at Husaby Kristin wins the respect of all her housefolk through her kindness and fair treatment, and with the welfare of her sons ever in mind she makes every effort to regain some of the possessions which Erlend has forfeited to crown and church through the wanton behavior of his youth. A certain feeling of peace comes over her. However, she soon realizes that there is no permanence to her heart-felt contrition. Too many responsibilities rest upon her shoulders with all the everyday problems of managing the estate and caring for the seven sons she has born Erlend as well as for Erlend's two children by Eline. It is not in Erlend's nature to concern himself with problems of home and manor. He cannot tolerate talk of husbandry and housefolk and tenants and young ones. His world lies outside among men and in the affairs of state. He is a man of unquestioned courage, but quick-tempered and headstrong and prepared to venture anything, unmindful of the consequences. Erlend can do harm through his thoughtlessness, but he is incapable of a mean impulse nor can he harbor any grudge. Kristin, on the other hand, is unable to forget any wrong done her, and it is because of her own stubbornness and defiance that Erlend is driven to an act of unfaithfulness.

Tensions arise between the two, so that Erlend can no longer, as formerly, come forward to beg forgiveness for his hot temper, for he notices that Kristin is lacking in all wifely gentleness and forbearance. He confronts her with the charge: "It is not from holiness, Kristin, that you are always tearing open these old sins of ours, but it is to have a weapon to use against me every time I oppose you in anything." [18]

Kristin understands the truth of these words. She thinks to herself:

It was not that she wilfully or with malice aforethought stored up grudges against her husband. She knew that she was not petty-minded toward others, but toward Erlend she was so at the least provocation. When Erlend was involved, she could forget nothing, and every least scratch on her soul went on smarting and bleeding and swelling and throbbing, when it was he that had given it to her. [19]

Despite these tensions Kristin loves Erlend dearly, for she has chosen him herself and in doing so she has placed her personal desires above the love of her father and her family. She has chosen a life of turmoil rather than give up the golden garland and the pleasures of the world proffered her by the elf-maiden.

When Erlend is imprisoned and charged with treason for his unsuccessful attempt to deprive King Magnus of his land and throne in favor of Haakon Knutsson, Kristin realizes that Erlend has taken up a cause so great that none of the other chieftains had dared to set a hand to it. In Erlend's worst hour Kristin reveals the true depth of her love. A. H. Winsnes compares Kristin to Gudrun in *The Laxdoela Saga* and to Vigdis in Sigrid Undset's *Gunnar's Daughter,* for like them she too treats most cruelly the very man she loves most dearly. [20]

Through Simon's intercession Erlend has been released from prison and now at the beginning of the third part of the novel, *Korset* (*The Cross*), Kristin and Erlend return to Jörundgaard. Because of his act of treason Erlend has forfeited the right to his family manor at Husaby and must now be satisfied to live on his wife's estate at Jörundgaard, which has fallen to her after her parents' death. When Kristin was living at Husaby, she had fond memories of her happy youth spent at Jörundgaard. Now her thoughts go back to the great household at Husaby with all the serving folk and the din when Erlend's men came riding into the

courtyard with clashing arms. She knows how Erlend longs for
the broad expanse of fields and meadows, the shores of the nearby
fjord with wharves and ships and the smell of tar and fishing gear
and the excitement of the market town with its churches and
cloisters and feasts in great men's houses. In the Dale where the
landowners are closely allied by marriage and fellowship Erlend
has no friends. People cannot forget that this haughty Trondheim
chieftain had plotted to raise rebellion against his king.

Despite these difficulties Erlend seems to have become more
readily reconciled to the new circumstances than Kristin, and to
all outward appearances he is quite content. A carefree spirit,
fickle and irresponsible, he is capable of accepting the bad together with the good. He likes to roam about in the woods in the
company of his sons and hunt down wild beasts, but to Kristin it
seems that he would do better to train his young sons in husbandry, now that there is small hope for them in the knightly
calling. She feels that her sons are gradually being drawn away
from her by Erlend and that they are not interested in learning
anything of the ways of the parish and its folk. Even she has become a stranger in her own home country. Like a noble chieftain
Erlend can carry on with head unbowed when misfortune strikes,
but Kristin cannot accept ill fortune and loss of prestige that easily. In her self-righteousness she believes that she alone has had all
the toil and struggle of saving her heritage and raising her children and establishing a firm groundwork on which their fortunes
may again be built up. She is unrelenting and stubborn in her
demands, and although she has sworn that she will never express
any words of reproach to Erlend for his misdeeds, she finds it
difficult to hide her despair at his eternal heedlessness.

Sometimes she vents her wrath on her madcap sons, because
they prefer to lead their own lives and are not as tractable as she
would wish. She knows that she is stubborn and selfish, but she is
unable to follow her father's admonition: "He who with contrite
heart is mindful of his sins and bows down before the Lord's
cross, will never have to bend his neck before this world's misfortune or injustice." [21] She must bear to hear Erlend say: "Often
when you speak so softly and sweetly as though your mouth were
filled with honey, I am afraid you are thinking more of old
wrongs. May God judge whether your heart is as pious as your
mouth." [22] In a violent outburst of anger Kristin rebukes Erlend:

"You console yourself with the thought, Erlend, as you sit there in my father's high-seat, that your sons shall be saved by his prayers, just as they are fed by his lands," and then she adds: "He was—a better master—he who—sat there before you." [23]

Erlend can no longer endure to live with Kristin and moves to a small abandoned croft in the Dovre mountains, the only piece of land he still owns by lawful deed. After some time Kristin at the urging of Simon visits her husband in an attempt at reconciliation. However, Erlend knows that no good will come of his return to Jörundgaard. Here in the mountains he feels like a free man, but he knows he counts for little elsewhere. He bids her stay with him for he has always loved her, whether he did her good or evil. Kristin, however, cannot leave her children, even though they are beginning to lead their own independent lives. As she leaves, Erlend says: "You know well, Kristin—whether you come by night or by day—whether I wait for you for a long time or a short time—I shall always welcome you as though you were the Queen of Heaven come down to my croft from the skies." [24]

Erlend and Kristin have come to the parting of the ways; Erlend remains in his dilapidated shack in the mountains, but Kristin returns to Jörundgaard. There she gives birth to another son, her eighth, and has the boy christened Erlend after its father. Even as she gives the child this name, it is as though she were breaking all ties which bind her to him who bears this same name.[25] She has not forgiven Erlend, even though she kneels in church and prays: "Forgive us our trespasses as we forgive those that trespass against us." She promises God that she will say this prayer without guile and think of her husband with peace in her soul, but this is more than she can do. Her own sins have been forgiven her again and again, but she cannot find it in her heart to forgive Erlend, whom she once loved so tenderly. As she whispers the words: "Sicut et nos dimittimus debitoribus nostris" she feels "her hand harden like a hand that is clenched for a blow." [26] Erlend Erlendsson dies shortly after, scarcely three months old.

Erlend returns to the district to defend Kristin against the charge that a house servant and not he was the father of her child, and in protecting her honor is slain by an angry mob. The scene which leads up to Erlend's death presents the dramatic climax to the love story of Kristin and Erlend. Since the day they met in Oslo a passionate love had dominated their lives and determined their fates. In his dying words Erlend gives the key to the tragedy of their love. " 'Kiss me, Kristin,' he whispered. There was just a shade of laughter in his voice. 'There has been too much else between you and me—than the Christian religion and wedlock—that we can now easily—take leave of one another—as Christian man and wife.' " [27]

To his sons he explains that whatever ill blood has ever existed between their mother and himself was caused by him, and that their mother has always loved them more than her own life. Erlend refuses to accept the last rites from a priest who was among those who had slandered Kristin. He dies like a pagan hero of old with a smile on his lips, but because he can forgive Kristin and take upon himself all blame for the troubled years they have experienced together, he seems better prepared than Kristin to stand in the presence of God.

The novel could have ended at this point. It would have been a great realistic novel of the Middle Ages with its light focused on the instincts and passions which are stronger than human reason and which inexorably lead men to their tragic end. However, *Kristin Lavransdatter* is more than just such a realistic novel. It is a religious work which is concerned not with man's heart, but with his soul, and the victory of the soul over the flesh. It is not an easy victory, for Sigrid Undset has an open eye to man's sensual nature. Her most finely drawn characters are those men and women of flesh and blood who are torn between the two irreconcilable poles of human will and divine will. The religious theme comes into sharper focus in the last part of *The Cross* as Kristin renounces the world with its strife and turmoil and finds final peace and harmony as she bows before God and accepts His divine grace.

After Erlend's death some of the bitterness which Kristin has always stored in her heart seems to disappear. She continues to concern herself greatly with the welfare of her sons. A certain peace of mind comes over her as she fondles her first grandchild and thinks back on all the joys she has had from her own children. It pleases her that her son Gaute, who has taken over the estate at Jörundgaard after his marriage, is as openhanded as all her other sons, for she believes that those who hold their udal lands should strive to increase their goods and waste nothing, but at the same time should always give generously of their store to all wayfarers who beg alms in the name of God. Formerly she always prayed to God that He might grant her every wish. She never came to God with her sins as long as there was any sweetness in life for her enjoyment. To Erlend's brother, the monk Gunnulf, she says: "Disobedience was the chief of my sins, Gunnulf—and I was unsteadfast, too. All the days of my life I have longed both to go the right way and at the same time to go astray on my own wayward paths." [28]

Kristin gets along very well with Jofrid, Gaute's wife, but she now no longer rules as mistress of the estate, nor can she give advice and counsel, as she always has in the past. Love for Erlend has always been the very essence of her existence, and now that he is dead, life can have no further meaning for her. She decides to leave Jörundgaard and once again journey on the pilgrim's path to Nidaros. She wishes to be present at the festival of St. Olav and then seek admission to the convent at Rein.

As she wanders over the Dovre mountains she looks back upon her entire past life and begins to see everything in a new perspective. It is as though she were standing upon the heights and looking down into the valley below. She is given the grace to understand that in like fashion does God view His creation and look into the hearts of all men with their sins and sorrows and their loves and their hates. Man in his short span of life from birth to death is but a small part of this divine order. Kristin examines herself in this new light. She has hurried through a turbulent and reckless life fighting with ungoverned spirit against every obstacle placed in her path. She has loved God, although not as much as her own will; yet God has helped her every time she has prayed in her anguish and sorrow. His mercy has been so great that despite her stubborn will she has been able to catch some reflection of the heavenly light.

Kristin is received by the sisters of the convent at Rein, and it is her intent to become a professed nun after the required two years of probation. When the Black Death breaks out in 1349 and rages with particular violence at Nidaros and at the convent at Rein, Kristin dedicates herself with all humility to the care of the sick and dying, for in this time of dire need she feels that all mankind is brought closer together as children of God. She saves a young boy from the hands of ungodly men who are about to offer him as a sacrifice to the pagan goddess of Hel in order that they may be spared the ravages of the pestilence. With her own hands she bears into hallowed ground the body of the boy's mother who has died of the plague and has been denied a Christian burial because of her sinful life. Kristin too becomes a victim of the dread disease, and on her death-cot she offers her bridal ring to God. On her middle finger where the ring had been, she sees a mark which looks like an M, the first letter of the Virgin's holy name. She now understands what has always seemed like a mystery she could not fathom:

God had held her fast in a covenant made for her without her knowledge by a love poured out upon her richly—and despite her self-will, despite her heavy earthbound spirit, something of this love had become *part* of her, had worked within her like sunlight in the earth, had brought forth a yield which not even the hottest flames of carnal love nor its wildest bursts of wrath could lay waste entirely. A handmaiden of God she had been—a wayward, unruly servant, most often giving lip service in her prayers and faithless in her heart, being slothful and negligent, impatient under reproach, little constant in her tasks—yet He had held her fast in His service, and under the glittering golden ring on her finger a mark had been set upon her secretly, showing that she was His handmaiden, owned by the Lord and King who was now coming, borne by the priest's anointed hands, to give her freedom and salvation.[29]

All of Sigrid Undset's works, both her medieval novels and her novels of modern life, are concerned with that sense of responsibility given to all men to further the welfare of their fellow men to the extent of their special abilities. This feeling of responsibility stems from her belief in the universal brotherhood of mankind, and it extends from the loyalty required of the individual in his relationship to his fellow man on this earth to a transcendental loyalty to his Creator. In her contemporary novels she denounced the lack of loyalty in the liberal philosophies and collective movements of a materialistic age which would do away with all religion. It was in the medieval period that she saw the individual come to grips with his Christian faith, for even as he was emerging from paganism he felt the need for worship of some outside force, be it in the form of nature worship or even in the practice of witchcraft. The medieval Christian was without doubt very often disloyal in his faith. However, the conflict of conscience which resulted from his disloyalty indicates that he was fully aware of his wrongdoing, but at the same time unable to subordinate his will to the will of a higher supernatural order. This is the nature of Kristin's conflict, and it applies just as well to Olav Audunssön, the main figure of Sigrid Undset's other medieval novel. It is only after an entire lifetime of struggle and inner torment that both are able to break loose from the mesh of their selfish interests and find peace and harmony in a theocentric philosophy of life.

Not so with Kristin's father Lavrans or with Simon to whom Kristin has been betrothed. Neither is faced with such a conflict for both are able to bear without murmur the burdens which have been laid upon them. God has brought great sorrow to Lavrans. He has taken his children from him one by one; first his three sons, then his daughter Ulvhild, and then Kristin whom he has loved most of all. The trust that he has in his wife Ragnfrid and his daughter Kristin is put to a severe test, but Lavrans never wavers in his faith and devotion to both. He thinks of Kristin as the little fair-haired maid who always followed him about so lovingly, and he wishes that God may reward her for all the joy she has given him. For his wife Ragnfrid, too, he has only kind thoughts, even though there has been no complete happiness in their marriage.

As a youth Lavrans had been of a mind to take monastic vows, and when he had been out fishing in the Botn Fjord and had heard the bells ringing from the monastery on Hovedö, it had seemed that they were drawing him closer and closer. However, he had given up this wish in order not to displease his father. In speaking to Kristin he reveals the whole purpose of his life. He says:

> I have felt it more and more each year that I have lived—there can be no worthier work for a human soul that has found grace to understand a little of God's mercy, than to serve Him and watch and pray for those men whose sight is still darkened as they walk in the shadow of the things of this world. Yet must I say, my Kristin, it would have been hard for me to give up for God's sake the life I have lived on my lands, with cares for earthly things and with worldly pleasure—with your mother at my side, and with you my children. Therefore a man who has begotten offspring of his body must suffer in patience lest his heart break if he should lose them or if they fare badly in this world. God, who gave them souls, owned them, and not I.[30]

These words of Lavrans are far removed from the wild fury of the Viking period and of the spirit of revenge of the pre-Christian aristocratic family society. They echo some of the gentle tones of the Norwegian didactic and religious literature of the thirteenth century and thus give a good indication of the extent to which Christianity had become a living force in the minds of men of that time.

Simon, a man of the greatest humility, likewise finds a source of great strength in his Christian faith, and it is interesting to compare his kindness with Kristin's selfish behavior. After the marriage pact with Kristin has been broken, Simon marries Ramborg, Kristin's younger sister, and as a kinsman he does all in his power to be of help to Kristin and Erlend in their many difficulties. Through the years Simon remains constant in his faithful devotion to Kristin, even though she has rejected him for the sake of Erlend's love.

From the man she had rejected she had taken help every time it was a question of saving the man of her choice. The suitor she had cast aside was the man she had turned to each time she needed a protection for her love. And she had never asked Simon for anything in vain—time after time he had stepped forward to protect her with his kindness and his strength.[31]

Kristin is grateful to Simon, but she cannot rid herself of the thought that she has suffered humiliation, because she has not been able to repay him for all the kindness and favors he has always shown her. An opportunity is presented in the serious illness of Simon's young son Andres. In his despair Simon begs Kristin for her help in saving the boy's life, and when no other remedy avails, she suggests that they resort to witchcraft, the knowledge of which she has learned from Lady Aashild, Erlend's aunt. However, the final decision to take such extreme measures she leaves in Simon's hands, and Simon, because he loves the child so dearly, gives his tacit consent.

Under cover of darkness Kristin steals into the churchyard to cut a piece of turf from a grave. She knows that she is committing a sinful and unchristian deed, for she is attempting to turn aside God's hand, when He would stretch it forth to take a living soul. Sorcery seemingly saves the boy's life, but Kristin has not given her help out of any spirit of kindness. She recalls an earlier occasion in Oslo when Simon had been witness to her shame, and she can never forget that in the confrontation of Simon and Erlend it was Simon who had shown that he was worthier than the man she loved. Now she has been able to save the boy's life and thus return in some measure the kindness shown her, but even more important, she has seen Simon at that one moment in his life when his faith in God wavered, and she can derive some satisfaction from the fact that he must know that she shares this secret with him.

For the modern reader, however, there is much more in the novel than the description of such mental conflicts or of the impact which religious thinking had upon the conduct of men at that time, as interesting as such analyses may be. Sigrid Undset was very much interested in the cultural history of her native land and through extensive research was able to gather an immense store of knowledge about the people and conditions of life in Norway during the Middle Ages. No area of life is left untouched in her powerful and realistic description of people and places. Her subjects range from the simple parish stave-church to the awe-inspiring cathedral of Trondheim, from the pious beggar monk and the plain chapter house to the learned bishop and the palace at Hamar. She describes church festivals and processions and draws word pictures of life within the walls of monasteries and convents. Three articles which she contributed to a cultural-historical volume on Norway testify to her great interest in this material.[32] These articles together with her study *Norske helgener* (*Saga of Saints*) supplement the material of which she makes use in her medieval novels.[33] They offer fascinating and highly informative reading and are most valuable for a better understanding of the viewpoints and attitudes revealed in her novels.

Medieval life included also the hard-working husbandman's daily struggle for existence. The descriptions of the Norwegian manor and of the many family activities as they unfold within the framework of the society of that day are features of Sigrid Undset's two medieval novels which have enduring appeal to every reader. The notes to the English translation of *Kristin Lavransdatter* are equipped with two diagrams. One is a plan of Jörundgaard with its dwelling-houses, workshops, storehouses, and servants' quarters situated around the courtyard, and the farm-buildings with barn, cowsheds, pigsties and sheep-pens encircling the farm-yard, and the stable separating the two yards. Located at some distance in the fields were the smithy and the bathhouse. The other diagram shows a typical hearthroom-house with benches and tables, beds and closets, and porch and lofts. The description of Jörundgaard reminds one of Maihaugen, the open-air museum at Lillehammer with its seventeenth-century farm buildings from Björnstad, or the Norwegian folk museum at Bygdöy in Oslo with its many old buildings assembled from various sections of medieval Norway.

The novel presents an intimate picture of family life within the walls of these buildings. One sees the women preparing food and drink, mending clothes, and decorating walls and tables as they await the arrival of kinsmen and friends for Yule or wedding celebration. We see the children playing on the floor of the hearthroom or following in the footsteps of the father outside in the courtyard as he goes about giving orders to the servants or busying himself with the many tasks requiring his attention.

Sigrid Undset draws a complete picture of the course of human life, from the labor pains of the mother giving birth to her child to the garbled sounds of the dying man as the priest administers the last rites. She is able to identify with the characters of her novel, so that she can experience with them the whole range of their human emotions. She includes not only the simple folk cultivating their lands in the valley or tending their flocks on the mountain-side, but also the great landowners and the members of the lower nobility in the large manor houses, the shoemakers and the silver-smiths in their dingy shops in the narrow city streets and even the retinue of the king's residence in Oslo.

All these figures and their actions are seen against the background of the Norwegian landscape changing from season to season in rhythmic pattern. Sigrid Undset loved the beauties of her native land. As a child she spent never-to-be-forgotten summers north of the Dovre mountains in Tröndelag at the home of her paternal grandparents. The family spent other summers in the Österdal valley or resorts closer to Oslo such as Dröbak or Hvit-sten. She knew Nordmarka and Gudbrandsdal very well from hiking trips during holiday seasons. From her spacious house at Lillehammer where she lived for about twenty years she had a glimpse of beautiful Lake Mjösa to the south. Above all, it was the mountains which had a particular fascination for her, as may be seen in the many passages in all her works describing the beauties of such scenery. There is something timeless about the natural beauty of this country. As Sigrid Undset writes about the fjords, the mountains, the lakes, and the towns in their medieval setting, she is at the same time describing the very same scenery and places with which the modern Norwegian is already familiar. Through the centuries the landscape has changed just as little as the people themselves. A certain quality of reality is therefore given to the work through reference to such well-known place names as the Dovre mountains, Österdal, Gudbrandsdal, Lake Mjösa, or Oslo, Nidaros (Trondheim), Björgvin (Bergen), Hamar, Akersnes, Tunsberg, Romerike, and dozens of others.

The impression of reality is furthermore increased by the accuracy of the historical setting, particularly in the second part of the novel, to a lesser extent in the third part, and only very incidentally in the first part, which contains more of the spirit of the folk song or ballad. The action in the second part covers the years from 1319, when Haakon V died, until the mid-thirties. Haakon V was succeeded as king of Norway by his grandson Magnus, who was the son of Duke Eirik of Sweden and Ingebjörg, the daughter of Haakon V. Magnus thus became king of a dual monarchy, since he had already become king of Sweden in 1318 with the slaying of Duke Eirik by his brother King Birger and the subsequent expulsion of the king. During Magnus' minority Councils were established in the two countries and Ingebjörg had a position of importance in both Councils. She abused this power in favor of Knut Porse, the Danish knight, who as leader of the army had driven out King Birger and later married Ingebjörg in 1326. In 1322 the nobles of Sweden took the power out of Ingebjörg's hands, and in 1323 the Norwegian nobles under the leadership of Archbishop Eiliv did likewise. Erling Vidkunsson, who was to rule with the assistance of the Council of Nobles, was appointed High Steward of Norway.

When Magnus became of age in 1330 Sir Erling resigned, but when the young king remained in Sweden and left Norway without any government, the nobles headed by Erling Vidkunsson and Jon and Sigurd Haftorsson, cousins of the young king, planned to depose him. They were threatened with severe penalties, but managed to come to terms with the king, who then appointed a new High Steward and strengthened the powers of the Council.

All these facts are woven into the fabric of the novel. Erlend's plot against Magnus on the other hand is an invented episode. In the novel Erlend planned to bring Haakon Knutsson, the son of Ingebjörg and Knut Porse, to Norway and later force Magnus to give his young half-brother the kingship of Norway. He believed that the Norwegian people were at a severe disadvantage because of the fact that Magnus had scarcely ever set foot on Norwegian soil and had shown unwillingness to set up any appropriate government. Because of his wastefulness in money matters the people were being unduly taxed. It was difficult for the Norwegians to receive the same justice as Swedish knights, and it was only to be expected that a man like the young king, unskilled in affairs of state as he was, should pay more heed to his Swedish lords and thus be more considerate of them than of his Norwegian subjects.

Though Erlend was found guilty of treason, he had acted out of a conviction that he was carrying out the wishes of most people. At that time there was great opposition to Magnus in all quarters, and Erlend without doubt expected a greater following of men to support him. Had he been successful in his attempt to put Haakon on the throne, a lasting peace might have been established in Norway, and the laws and customs of the land as handed down from time immemorial might have been upheld. Furthermore, it had always been considered the right of the Norwegian farmers and chieftains to set aside a king who had tried to rule unlawfully.

The details of the plot are not made all too clear in the novel. It is certain that Erlend was not the only one involved. Others, however, were able to extricate themselves from the danger and escape unharmed. Erlend alone has to suffer, but even when he is put on the rack of torture he refuses to implicate others. To Simon he says that "he had promised all who had allied themselves with him that he would hold the rope, so that if worst came to worst, the blow should fall on his hands alone." [34] Never did Erlend betray anyone who put his trust in him.

As mentioned above, the story of Erlend's plot was invented by Sigrid Undset. Needless to say, Erlend himself and Kristin and most of the chief figures of the novel are also completely fictitious characters. The Regent Erling Vidkunsson, to be sure, is a historical figure, as is Duke Knut Porse. However, the latter does not actually appear in the novel, although the political action does revolve around him. Many other names in *Kristin Lavransdatter,* such as Munan Baardsson, Erlend's cousin, are also known from documents of the time, but it is only through Sigrid Undset's novel that they have come to life as historical personalities.

On the whole the historical circumstances as described in the novel are basically correct. Scholars such as Fredrik Paasche and Yngvar Hauge acknowledge that all characters and events which Sigrid Undset invented have parallels in historical reality. Nevertheless, in spite of her profound knowledge of Norway's medieval past Sigrid Undset has not written a "historical novel," because she was not by far as interested in the external facts of history as in the inner lives of the men and women of that age. In writing of a period in Norwegian history for which written documents are very scarce, Sigrid Undset was able to give freer rein to her poetic imagination. She has been able to create the illusion of reality, so that Victor Vinde can write: "She has breathed the breath of life into the creatures of her imagination. Few characters in literature are as truly alive as Kristin Lavransdatter; here is no wax figure but a woman of flesh and blood. She is also an entirely probable historical character. Who can doubt that she actually lived during the epoch so empty of record which . . . henceforth must be known as the epoch of Kristin Lavransdatter!" [35]

II Olav Audunssön

Sigrid Undset's second novel of medieval life appeared in two volumes: *Olav Audunssön i Hestviken* (*Olav Audunssön of Hestviken*) in 1925 and *Olav Audunssön og hans börn* (*Olav Audunssön and His Children*) in 1927. In this novel the action takes place in the second half of the thirteenth century and the early part of the fourteenth century, that is, during the generation which precedes that of Kristin Lavransdatter. It is the time of Magnus Law-Mender and of his sons, Eirik and Haakon V. The novel also describes the invasion of Norway in 1308 by another Eirik, Duke

Eirik of Sweden, who was later to marry Princess Ingebjörg, the
daughter of Haakon V.

In the novel we hear echoes of the civil war between King
Sverre's "Birchlegs" ("Birkebeinere"), the opponents of the
Church, and the "Bagler" or "Crozier Men" under King Magnus
Erlingsson. The conflict was continued between King Haakon IV,
the son of King Haakon III, and Duke Skule who claimed the
crown after the death of his brother King Inge Baardsson.
Haakon IV with the support of the "Birchlegs" defeated Duke
Skule at the Battle of Oslo and with the slaying of Skule by the
"Birchlegs" in 1240 the civil war came to an end. Sigrid Undset
mentions that Audun, Olav's father, and Steinfinn, Ingunn's fa-
ther, both served in the bodyguard of King Haakon IV, and that
Steinfinn was at the king's bedside when he died at Kirkwall in
the Orkneys in 1263.

Political events, however, exist only at the periphery of most
men's lives, and although they present a fitting background for the
period described, they have little relevance to the action of the
novel or to the development of the religious and psychological
problems formulated in it.

The scene of the novel is laid for the most part at Hestviken on
the Oslo Fjord, the ancestral home of Olav Audunssön, and at
Frettastein on Lake Mjösa, the home of Ingunn, Steinfinn's
daughter. The reader is also given interesting descriptions of conditions in Denmark, where Olav lives for some time as an outlaw
at the home of his maternal uncle, and in medieval London,
which he visits on a trading mission.

As children Olav and Ingunn have been betrothed to one another by their fathers, and after the death of his parents Olav is
fostered by Steinfinn at Frettastein. Olav and Ingunn grow up
together almost as brother and sister. For the most part they are
free to play and roam about the manor as they please, for Steinfinn and his wife Ingebjörg give little thought to the care of the
children. The only religious instruction which the children receive
comes from Brother Vegard of Hamar who visits Frettastein twice
a year as their father confessor. Neglected as they are by everyone
at Frettastein the children find comfort in each other's company.

A boat trip which the teen-age boy and girl take to Hamar
one summer day is described with a freshness and buoyancy
which is not to be found elsewhere in the entire novel. The tender

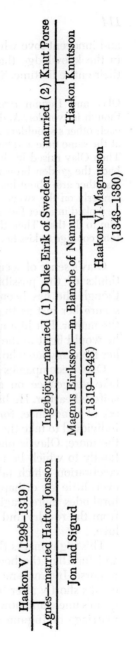

KINGS OF NORWAY

Magnus Erlingsson (1162–1184)

Sverre (1184–1202)

Haakon III (1202–1204)

Inge Baardsson (1204–1217)

Haakon IV the Old (1217–1263)

Magnus Law-Mender (1263–1280)

Eirik Priest-Hater (1280–1299)   Haakon V (1299–1319)

                                       Ingebjörg

RULERS OF SWEDEN AND NORWAY

Birger Jarl

Magnus III (1275–1290)

Birger II (1290–1319)   Duke Valdemar   Duke Eirik—married Ingebjörg (Haakon V of Norway)

                                       Magnus Eiriksson (1319–1343)

DESCENDANTS OF HAAKON V

Haakon V (1299–1319)

Agnes—married Haftor Jonsson   Ingebjörg—married (1) Duke Eirik of Sweden   married (2) Knut Porse

Jon and Sigurd   Magnus Eiriksson (1319–1343)—m. Blanche of Namur   Haakon Knutsson

                                       Haakon VI Magnusson (1343–1380)

and innocent love which is kindled in their hearts is strengthened
in the knowledge that they are destined to remain together for
their entire lifetime. Sigrid Undset writes:

Olav and Ingunn remained on their knees, facing each other, as
though in wonder. And without saying a word they laid their arms on
each other's shoulders and leaned forward close together. They let go
at the same time and looked at each other with a faint smile of surprise.
Then Olav raised his hand and touched the girl's temples. He pushed
back the golden brown disheveled hair. As she let him do it, he put
his other arm about her, drew her toward him, and kissed her long and
tenderly on the sweet, tempting pit under the roots of the hair. Then
he looked into her face and a warm tingling ran through him—she liked
him to do that. Then they kissed each other on the lips, and at last he
took courage to kiss her on the white arch of her throat.[36]

Olav's sense of security, however, begins to be shaken, when he
thinks of the possibility that he might yet lose Ingunn, even
though she has been promised to him. He would now wish to
secure her just as the serving-men take the coarse womenfolk at
the manor. For him no future without Ingunn is conceivable, and
he would fight to the death to have her as his own and to protect
her from anyone who would stretch out his hand toward her.

Olav accompanies his foster-father Steinfinn as he sets out to
take vengeance on an enemy for a humiliation which he has
suffered earlier. He has no moral scruples about taking part in this
act of vengeance, for it is a generally accepted practice for the
individual to take the execution of justice into his own hands. Furthermore, Olav is playing out his part as a loyal kinsman of the
family to which he now feels indissolubly bound. At the victory
celebration which takes place later at Frettastein there is, however, little joy or happiness, but rather a tense atmosphere which
forebodes more tragic happenings. Olav and Ingunn steal away
from the revelry and give themselves over to their all-consuming
love.

This night marks the end of the happy years of their childhood
and for Olav the beginning of an entire lifetime of anguish and
remorse. Ingunn's mother dies during the night and Steinfinn suc-
cumbs shortly after to the wounds suffered in battle. Kolbein, Ingunn's uncle and now her guardian, and other kinsmen oppose the
marriage of Ingunn to Olav, for they know that they will have

need of a stronger and more powerful ally than this young stripling of sixteen years, if they are to maintain a position of strength against their enemies in the family feud which is now certain to break out. Furthermore, there are no witnesses to testify that Ingunn was in fact betrothed to Olav, now that Steinfinn and Audun, Olav's father, are both dead. Nevertheless, Olav considers the agreement binding and is determined to make Ingunn his wife.

Upon the advice of his loyal friend Arnvid, a kinsman of Ingunn, Olav pleads his case before Bishop Torfinn at Hamar. The bishop explains that Ingunn and Olav took an obligation upon themselves in that they did not give notice of their marriage in the presence of kinsmen nor by the proclamation of church banns. However, since they have lived together, they have thereby given consent to the betrothal arranged by their parents and are now bound to live together until death, or else to remain single, if a reconciliation with Ingunn's kinsmen cannot be effected. In any case, neither is free to marry any other without falling into the sin of adultery. The bishop adds that Olav must attempt to make a satisfactory settlement with Ingunn's uncles, for in the present circumstances Ingunn has certainly forfeited her rights to dowry and inheritance. Furthermore, he must also do penance publicly, because he has made his marriage in secret, whereas it should have been made in the open and in seemly fashion. Olav is not completely honest with Arnvid or Bishop Torfinn, for he does not confess that it was not merely out of obedience to their fathers' agreement that Ingunn and he had stolen into the bridal bed.

Nevertheless, events seem to be taking a favorable turn until Olav in a fit of rage slays Einar, Kolbein's son, for his vile and slanderous remarks. Olav is put under arrest, and now the old law of the family society, which allows for and even demands private revenge, stands in direct confrontation with the law of the State, which has taken from the individual the right of such enforcement. On this point the Church supported the State; it would punish lawbreaking according to the law and not with fresh deeds of unlawfulness which beget further acts of vengeance without end. Haftor, Einar's brother, who is prevented from taking the law into his own hands, remarks: "I call them dirty laws, these new laws. The old ones were better suited to men of honor—but it is true the new ones are better suited for such fellows as Olav there, who outrage the daughters of our best families and strike down their kinsmen when they call them to account for their misdeeds." [37]

Olav is imprisoned but escapes to Sweden and later travels to Denmark where he lives for some time with his mother's brother. In time he makes a money payment as partial atonement for the slaying of Einar and seems to be well on the way to a reconciliation with Haftor, who is far more reasonable in his terms of settlement than his father had been. Olav takes service in the retinue of a Swedish lord, for under the ban of outlawry he must continue to live abroad. His return home is thus delayed almost ten years.

Shortly before the end of Olav's years of exile Ingunn is seduced by Teit, a runaway Icelandic priest. Upon his return to Norway Olav learns from Ingunn's own lips that she no longer considers herself worthy of being his wife. Although furious with rage, Olav does not waver for a moment in his determination to remain loyal to Ingunn, the friend of his childhood, and to protect her in her shame and distress. He is even prepared to claim paternity of Ingunn's child by Teit, so that the misfortune may be hidden forever. Olav finds that he can forgive Ingunn, for through the grace of God all wicked thoughts of her are removed from his heart. He realizes that Ingunn is a weak and fragile creature and he swears that he will not let her suffer, but will do everything in his power to take her burden from her.

As far as Teit is concerned, however, he has other thoughts. In order to avenge the wrong done to Ingunn and himself Olav must take the law into his own hands. He is soon given the opportunity to do so while traveling over a lonely mountain pass with Teit. After a bitter struggle Olav kills the ravisher of his wife and burns down the mountain hut where they had rested, so that no evidence of the murder can be found. Olav has now committed a sin far greater than the slaying of Einar. That blow was struck in open combat when he heard his friend Arnvid slandered. He has made the proper atonement for the wrong done and has made his peace with Ingunn's kinsmen without any loss of prestige to himself. The murder of Teit on the other hand is a dastardly deed. He gives no notice of the slaying at the first house he passes, so that the deed must be reckoned as secret murder rather than as manslaughter. Nor is he of any mind to make amends for the murder by payment of weregild or fine. Has he not merely done what any normal man would have done—kill his wife's paramour? He has slain many a brave man in honorable combat without feeling any pangs of conscience and he therefore sees no reason why he should be concerned with such a vagabond as Teit who has received nothing but his just due.

Had Olav confessed this murder, it is hardly likely that any legal action would have been taken against him. In that case, however, Ingunn's disgrace would have been bared for all the world to know. This is precisely what Olav would avoid, for he wishes to hold his head high among his peers and to protect Ingunn at any cost. His greatest desire is to return to Hestviken, which he has not seen since his childhood, and reestablish the manor there with the help of Ingunn. Hestviken lies far to the south, and there they will be able to start life anew, for no one else will have any knowledge of their past.

In the old family society Olav would not have been faced with any great problem. Even when he killed Einar he believed he had acted correctly even though impetuously. He was of much the same mind as Kolbein and Haftor. He thinks: "*All* men could never be such saints as to consent to submit all their concerns, great and small, to the judgment of their fellow Christians, always being satisfied with the law and with *receiving* their rights—never *taking* them for themselves." [38] It is only after the murder of Teit, however, that Olav realizes that he is not in conflict with his fellow men, but with God. Both Olav and Ingunn accept God as a living reality and honor and respect His Church upon earth, but they do not understand the extent of God's power of forgiveness. Indeed, Ingunn, aware of her great sin, even attempts suicide, because she knows that there can be no salvation for her after death. She has no thought of bargaining with God. She expects to be condemned to the fire of Hell, for she believes that punishment after sin is the natural and accepted order of all things.

For Olav, too, God is the Creator and rightful Lord. A priest, Brother Asbjörn, tells him: "It is easy, Olav, to be a good Christian as long as God asks no more of you than to hear sweet singing in church, and to be obedient to Him while He caresses you with the hand of a father." [39] The difficulty arises when God asks for more than Olav would give; when God's will is different from his own. As a Christian Olav knows that he must subordinate his relentless will to God's everlasting wisdom. Otherwise, as Bishop Torfinn has explained, it will surely happen that "the man who is

minded to do as he himself wills, will soon enough find out that he
has done that which he had never willed." [40]

Every human being has his rights in the face of God and no
one, not even a despicable wretch like Teit, is denied the help and
love of Christ, our Lord. This is the beginning of Olav's remorse.
He is aware of his sin, but he can never bring himself to confess it,
because he cannot bear to lose the respect accorded him by his
fellow men nor have Ingunn subjected to any shame. He swears
that he will never desert Ingunn nor will he ever make mention of
her transgression. Olav may well forgive Ingunn, for he is aware
of the fact that there are many wrongs for which he himself must
answer before God's judgment seat. But all this can wait. He feels
certain that an opportunity will come at some later time when he
will be able to make his peace with God on more favorable terms.

Because of the fines he has had to pay, Olav has been deprived
of all his possessions except his udal lands at Hestviken. Nevertheless, he is looked upon as a man of substance and honor in the
district where he had spent his childhood. Furthermore, he has a
sense of security and a feeling of fellowship with his father's relations, such as he had never known at Frettastein among Ingunn's
kinsmen. At Hestviken he feels that he can more easily bear the
burden of Ingunn's misfortune and his own sin. He lives piously,
practices charity, and honors the house of God, but he knows that
he is offering God only a makeshift, for he still has an unshriven
sin on his conscience. He works industriously on his farm, but he
is never free of the sudden assaults of a relentless remorse. Like
Kristin, Olav is torn between two forces. He too knows something
of the allurements of the elf-maiden. Sigrid Undset writes:

A conflict had been waged in the whole of Creation since the dawn of
the ages between God and His Enemy, and all that had life, soul, or
spirit took part in the battle in one host or the other—whether they
knew it or not—angels and spirits, men here on earth and beyond
death. And most often it was because of a man's own cowardice that
the Devil could entice him into his retinue—because the man was
afraid God might demand too much of him—command him to speak a
truth which was hard to force through his lips, or to abandon a cherished delight without which he didn't believe he was strong enough to
live: gain or welfare, wantonness or the respect of other people. Then
came the old Father of Lies and caught that man's soul with his old

master lie—that he demanded less of his servants and rewarded them better—as long as it lasted.[41]

But Olav cannot or will not give ear to this inner voice. Never would he receive absolution for his sin without public acknowledgment of the deed, so that justice might be done. He must choose in which host he will serve and he chooses to remain silent and to hide his sin and to carry the burden which he has fastened upon himself.

Life at Hestviken brings no happiness to Olav and Ingunn. They both consider it a punishment of God for their sins that Ingunn bears only stillborn children. To comfort his wife Olav has Eirik, her child by Teit, taken from its foster-mother and brought to Hestviken. Eirik is acknowledged by Olav as his own child and rightful heir, even though Ingunn later gives birth to a daughter, Cecilia. There is some love in his heart for Eirik and Cecilia, but Olav is so absorbed in his own remorse and unhappy fate that he is incapable of adjusting to new situations, and as a result his relationship to the children is strained almost to the breaking point. Eirik, to be sure, is a most complex nature, irresponsible, given to lies and incapable of carrying out any of the simple tasks assigned to him. At the same time he is devoted to Olav and longs for his love, but Olav can never be fair and just to the boy and rebuffs him at every turn. Cecilia, who was born after all happiness had already gone out of Olav's life, hates her father, because she recognizes the hardness of his heart. It is as though Olav's past has thrown up a wall between himself and his children. He cannot live at peace with them or with anyone else as long as he is not at peace with God.

Nor is there any happiness to be found in his marriage with Ingunn. It is true that not all Ingunn's misfortune is her own fault. She has had to suffer from a combination of unfortunate circumstances, not all of her own making. On the other hand, she is a weak-willed and self-centered person who has never made any effort to return the love which Olav has offered her. It is for her sake that Olav has Eirik brought to Hestviken, because he knows how much she longs for the child, and it is for her protection that he can never bring himself to confess his sin. Ingunn's sole concern is with her own lot and with the welfare of her son. She is

even jealous of her husband because of Eirik's obvious preference
for Olav in spite of her own efforts to win the boy's love through
indulgence. She cannot appreciate the fact that Olav has sacrificed his youth and health to bring her some measure of happiness
and she has no understanding of the turmoil which exists in his
heart. Indeed, it is primarily because of his love for Ingunn and
his deep sense of loyalty to her that he has been unable to make
his peace with God and bring rest to his tortured conscience. He
has known since childhood that she was lacking in judgment and
good sense, but God has given her into his care. "His love for her
was a habit, but it was also something very real; it was inter-
twined with his whole being as the soil of a meadow is inter-
twined with a mass of roots. But now he was beginning to feel
that this love was nothing more than an infinite compassion with
this poor sick creature whose life was his own life." [42]

There is a basic difference between Ingunn and her kinsmen on
the one hand and Olav on the other. For them "misfortune was
just like a poison they had swallowed. They held out until they
had thrown it up again—but then they died. . . . But he was
made of such stuff that he could endure even without happiness
. . . and if he got no happiness with her, since she could never
be anything but a sick and useless wife, that made no difference,
he now realized—he would love her and protect her to her last
hour." [43]

With the passing of time Olav becomes hardened in his sin. He
is given opportunities to make his confession, but he never finds
the courage to do so. It is as though a door were opened, but he
never dares to enter. And then the door is closed again. All the
time he must live at enmity with Christ, for he recognizes himself
as a liar and betrayer every time he enters His house. He says: "I
did not know that man could love God so much until I myself had
broken His covenant and lost Him!" [44]

To Arnvid's question as to why he does not make confession he
answers: "I cannot. . . I must think of Ingunn too—more than
of myself. I cannot condemn her to be left alone, broken in health,
poor and joyless, the widow of a base and cowardly murderer." [45]
He adds: "I long, day and night, to be reconciled with Christ, Our
Lord. . . . Never did our Saviour seem to me to be the source of
such infinite love until I learned that He had marked me with the
brand of Cain." [46]

Olav thinks that God is harder upon him than upon other men. He has seen men commit cruel deeds to which he would never have set his hand. Yet they seem to have enjoyed life and had a good death. But God pursues him, giving him no peace nor rest. Arnvid explains that God pursues him because He will not lose him. Furthermore, God's justice is not the same as man's. No two children of Eve does he treat alike. He does not demand the same fruits from all His children, to whom He has given such diverse talents.

At one time when Olav feels that he has found the courage to confess his sin, he expresses the wish to Ingunn that they travel to the altar of St. Olav at Nidaros and make amends for his offense against God and against the law and justice of his countrymen. Ingunn is terrified at the very thought of doing this, for she cannot bear to have men know of her shame and look upon her as a loose-minded man-mad thrall woman with a baseborn child begotten on her by a foreign vagabond. Ingunn stands out in glaring contrast to Olav. For her, even in her sickness, there is no solution except continued deception. She begs Olav to go on enduring for Eirik's sake and hers, even though it means that he must continue to live with a deadly sin burning in his soul. Ingunn is a woman almost devoid of any Christian faith. Olav, on the other hand, suffers the torments of anguish and remorse. He knows the way of God, but he has such a feeling of compassion for Ingunn, "this living bundle of pain," that he yields to her prayer and never broaches the subject again.

For years Olav has refused to give any thought to God's mercy. He has feared and fled so long from the justice of men that it seems unmanly and dishonorable to pray for this mercy now. Olav is honest enough to think that he has no right to elude the judgment of God, even though he has evaded men's justice. Now, however, he realizes that he has often been driven from the right road onto false paths, and yet God has always been prepared to take him back and restore him to grace. On the night before Ingunn's death he feels like one who has been snatched out of time and life on the very shore of eternity. He sees that the sin of all sins is to despair of God's mercy, for in spite of his sin and sorrow God has let him have his happiness in peace. The Lord has placed upon him the responsibility of caring for Ingunn, but Olav has looked upon this as a privilege. It is as though he has been taken by God from the paths of men and brought before His face. He feels closer to God than he has ever been before and he is resolved to fall at His feet and be raised up to Him.

The good resolution, however, is soon forgotten as soon as he begins to wonder about what will happen to the children. If he were to carry out his purpose, he would have to confess that he has pushed forward a bastard heir and thus cheated his nearest kinsmen at Frettastein of the family manor in favor of a stranger. He would have to make known the secret murder committed twelve years ago. He can well imagine how the Steinfinnsons would receive this news and how they would look upon Eirik. As atonement for his sin Olav would without doubt have to relinquish his rights to Hestviken and offer Cecilia as an oblate to the convent at Nonneseter with her mother's inheritance. Eirik, who had no rights whatsoever, he would have to send to the Preaching Friars. The race at Hestviken would die out, for there would be no one to carry on the line of which he was so proud and on which he has brought such misfortune. Thus Olav finds no relief for the sickness of his soul, because he does not feel he can jeopardize the lives of others.

After Ingunn's death Olav visits England on a trading voyage, and while abroad he has an experience which resembles that of Kristin Lavransdatter as she wanders over the Dovre mountains on her pilgrimage to Nidaros. At Hestviken Olav felt that there was too much he would have to give up to make amends for his sin: his honor, his welfare, his prestige, and even his life, but in England he feels the universality of the Church and the small role which one human soul plays in God's entire creation.

But now that he was in a place where he saw more of the splendor and riches of this world than he had believed could be collected in one spot—now all of a sudden everything that he called his own seemed to him so little—a man ought to be able to discard all this just as easily as he would hang his harp on the wall, when the battle trumpet called to arms. . . .

So he listened in calm meditation to the only voice that spoke to him in a tongue he understood—here in this foreign land, where all other voices shouted at him as though there were a wall between him and them. The voice of the Church was the same that he had listened to in his childhood and youth and manhood. He *had* changed—his aims and his thoughts and his speech, as he grew from one age into another; but the Church changed neither speech nor doctrine. It spoke to him in the Holy Mass as it had spoken to him when he was a little boy, . . . And he knew that if he traveled to the outermost limits of Christian men's habitation—the language and the customs of the people might indeed be strange and incomprehensible to him, but everywhere, when he came to a church and entered it, he would be welcomed by the same voice that had spoken to him when he was a child; with open hands the Church would offer him the same sacraments that she had nourished him with in his youth, and that he had rejected and misused.[47]

Olav feels that his role in life has been that of a Judas Iscariot. In the company of good Christians he alone has betrayed Christ. He has come of a line of ancestors who were loyal and unafraid, but he who in his youth gave every promise of upholding that honor, has broken the faith. Until this moment he has kept his apostasy hidden and has passed for a pious Christian, but now he will open his heart to God and all men.

The urgent need which he has to confess his sin, however, is once again forgotten upon his return to Hestviken. He begins to reason with himself that he was forced into his sin through the wrongs of other men. Had Ingunn's kinsmen not betrayed him and deprived him of his rights, he would not have been driven to take the steps which led to the ensnarement of one lie after another. It has been his bad lot to bear not only his own burdens but also those of others. His heart, on the other hand, tells him that he should have had the courage to acknowledge his youthful love for Ingunn; he should have had the strength to speak the truth and not concern himself with the judgment of those he loved.

Not until the very end of his life is Olav finally prepared to make his true confession. Now, however, he is partially paralyzed and unable to utter properly the words of the confession. It would seem that he has come to the end of a wasted life. He had been given the heritage of loyal, brave, and pious forebears, and God had marked him as a man who should have served as a model for all men. "He *should* have grown as the oak, patient and all-embracing, with protection and light for all who made their way to it. But as he was destined to grow, so did he grow—his inner cancer destroyed the marrow of his bones, so that he had become hollow, and withered and barren. He had not been able to protect anyone to any purpose." [48] He had longed to be a faithful warrior of God, "but here on earth it would never be his lot to see the radiance of a banner under which he might fight with the powers that were given him at his birth." [49]

In spite of this end of Olav's life there is a feeling of release in the heartfelt contrition and the joy which he experiences as he sees the sunrise one summer morning. In the glowing dawn he beholds the beauty and innocence of nature and the continuity in all God's creation. All nature rejoices in the Lord who has come to judge the world with righteousness.

He saw that they were now waiting, the trees that grew upon the rocks of his land, everything that sprouted and grew on his alodial land, the waves that followed one another in the bay—all were waiting to see judgment passed upon their faithless and disloyal master. It was this that the earth awaited every single hour, but it was in the trembling of dawn that the fair and betrayed earth sighed so that one heard it—sorrowful and merciless as a ravished maid it waited to be given justice against men, who went in, one by one, to the judgment seat. Every hour and every moment judgment was given; it was the watchword that one day called to another and one night whispered to the next. Everything that God had created sang the hymn of praise— *Benedicite omnia opera Domini Domino*—he too had known it when he was young. But those whom God had made chieftains and lords of the earth were false to Him and fought with one another, betraying Him and betraying their fellows.

Then the rays from the source of light broke out and poured down over him. For a moment he stared with open eyes straight into the eye of the sun, wild with love and longing, and he tried to gaze even deeper into God. He sank back in red fire, all around him there were glowing flames, and he knew that now the prison tower he had built around him was burning. But anointed by the glance that surrounded him he would walk out unharmed over the glowing embers of his burnt house, into the vision which is eternal bliss, and the fire that burned him was not as intense as his longing—.[50]

In this final vision Margaret Mary Dunn sees the logical culmination of a series of spiritual manifestations which are revealed to Olav through a lifetime of purgation.[51] In her new interpretation of *The Master of Hestviken* she points out that Olav time and again turns from the light because he does not have the courage to be loyal to his Christian commitment. However, Olav never rejects God. At no time is he guilty of what he considers the greatest sin: "to despair of God's mercy." He constantly nourishes the hope that he will at some time make amends to God for his unshriven sin.

Through moments of illumination or spiritual awakening, in which theme and structure coincide in a total artistic entity, Olav comes to acknowledge the magnitude of his guilt. Admission of his sin is itself a step toward purification, for it gives him renewed strength to take up again the burden of Ingunn as well as of Cecilia and Eirik, all of whom must depend upon him. Acceptance of this burden brings with it a lifetime of physical and mental suffering, not the least of which is the self-inflicted pain of his betrayal of the Lord. Olav's confession has been postponed, but only that his sorrow might deepen and that he might do full penance in this way for his unconfessed crime.

Toward the end of the novel we can observe the spiritual growth in Eirik's character. He seems to be making amends for Olav's own failure to be reconciled with God. This insight would seem to be confirmed by Eirik's own judgment of his foster-father, when he speaks to Cecilia after Olav's death:

We may not inquire into God's hidden counsels. Never will I believe it happened to father because his sin was worse than most men's. Maybe it was done to set forth an example—the rest of us give so little thought to our misdeeds. And God chose father to do full penance, because he saw into his heart—and knew that he was stronger and more faithful than we poor wretches who would not be able to swallow *one* drop of his justice. . . .[52]

Eirik is not really the "son avenger," in spite of the title of the last volume of the English translation; actually he is a responsible young husbandman, and Sigrid Undset means the reader to take his judgment seriously.

Like *Kristin Lavransdatter, Olav Audunssön* is a historical novel which has its setting in Norway of the Middle Ages. In many historical novels there is often a tendency to romanticize and idealize an age long since past and to present characters as the products of their specific time and milieu. This is not true of Sigrid Undset's novels. The chief characteristic of her historical novels is the synthesis which she has been able to make of that which is typical of any specific age and that which is universally human. She was, to be sure, absorbed in medieval studies since her childhood, and both novels are securely anchored in historical facts. With meticulous care she has created a pageant of the Middle Ages with all the color and detail accurately depicted. Nevertheless, it was not her purpose to recreate an era, but rather to present the historical events as a backdrop for the development of her individual characters. Hanna Astrup Larsen writes: "She has assimilated her scholarship so perfectly that she is able to write about people in the fourteenth century with the same wealth of realistic detail that she lavishes on her modern books. In this way she achieves a marvellously vivid background, but she never falls into the temptation of using her people as lay figures to drape in garments of historical fashion." [53]

Sigrid Undset is a realist not only in matters of external detail, but also in the exploration of the human heart. She does not attempt to idealize her characters, for she recognizes that they are people of flesh and blood with all their weaknesses and human frailties. She describes them just as they are, for better or for worse, and the reader believes in them, for they have the same joys and sorrows and doubts as men and women of our day.

Whether the historical events are correctly described or whether most of the characters in Sigrid Undset's novels had living counterparts is a matter of little importance. The borderline between truth and fiction is sometimes a very thin one. The Icelandic sagas, once thought to be an accurate documentation of historical events, are now considered for the most part to be pure fiction. They represent the work of creative artists who did, however, make use of all the historical facts available to them through a rich oral tradition. A. H. Winsnes writes: "The question whether the reality in her novels corresponds to actual historical conditions is, from a purely aesthetic point of view, quite superfluous. Literature has its own life, possesses an inner truth independent of historical fact. But respect for the material, the external matter from which her world is constructed, loyalty to tradition and accuracy in the treatment of fact—these, like her impressions of nature, are nonetheless an integral part in the process of artistic creation. The historical realism of these novels is inextricably bound up with their ethical and spiritual message of the eternal which dwells in every man and woman and her revelation of the common stuff of humanity which is colored, shaped and changed in the shifting tide of time." [54]

CHAPTER 5

The Later Novels

AFTER the completion of her two great medieval novels, *Kristin Lavransdatter* and *Olav Audunssön*, Sigrid Undset returned again to contemporary themes, this time in a series of novels in which the religious impulse is placed directly in the foreground. To be sure, the question of man's relationship to his Creator is, as we have seen, a theme central to the medieval novels too. This is not surprising, for in the Middle Ages the individual was conscious of the existence of a divine power beyond the visible world. Man might rise in defiance and set his self-will against God's supreme authority, but through God's redemptive grace he could again find salvation and be prepared for everlasting life. In accepting the dogmas of the Church and in recognizing the existence of a supernatural reality, medieval man possessed a solid metaphysical basis for all life.

In a world beset with confusion and conflicting interests, modern man has lost his faith in the vitality of Christianity. The "enlightened" mentality of the 1880's and 1890's saw in the church and Christianity forces hostile to the development of individual personality. Catchwords, such as "Progress," "Science," and "Evolution," to a great extent replaced all objective religious belief, and traditional and time-honored teachings were abandoned in favor of a cult of self-interest and a morality of success.

I   The Wild Orchid *and* The Burning Bush

It is the climate of such secularized liberalism which Sigrid Undset describes in her two doctrinaire novels *Gymnadenia* (*The Wild Orchid*) in 1929 and its sequel *Den brennende busk* (*The Burning Bush*) in 1930. In this novel cycle she tells of the conversion to Catholicism of Paul Selmer, the son of upper middle-class Protestant parents, who has been brought up in an unbelieving world, but who at the same time seeks to find some meaning in life amidst the shifting values about him. In Paul's prolonged struggle to find such an objective truth there is much that reflects Sigrid Undset's own development from an agnostic or freethinker to a believing Christian, so that the novel may be considered the most autobiographical of all her works.

Paul is one of four children of Julie Selmer, an "emancipated" woman of the Ibsen generation, who has divorced her husband, a conservative office manager, because there was no happiness in the marriage and because she refused to let herself be bound by old outworn principles about morality merely for the sake of keeping up appearances. Julie believes she has freed herself of all the conventional ideas and prejudices which were considered sacrosanct in her youth, but in doing so she has let herself be ensnared in the web of new prejudices and subjective opinions. She is a woman of intelligence and integrity, but there is a certain smugness in her show of tolerance, so that like most "enlightened" people she is most dogmatic and narrow-minded. They talk about a happy state of society when all people will be so far advanced that they will hold the same opinions as themselves. There is a warmth in their hearts, but their hearts are just the center of a tiny little circle, and instead of extending this circle they have actually wiped it out, "leaving behind merely a speck, the little ego, the heart which once was at any rate the center of a little sphere, within which it shed its warmth. Now this blessed warmheartedness merely radiates into empty space—people love this and that and the whole world in general—and nobody in particular, in the sense that they would make any big sacrifice for any individual person." [1]

His mother's scientific paganism and her spiritual sterility leave a large part of Paul's nature unsatisfied. He feels the need to objectify his religious belief, so that he might be able to return thanks to Someone outside the world for the beauty within it. The celebration on June 7, 1905, when the political union of Norway with Sweden was dissolved by the action of the Norwegian parliament, is a joyous occasion for all, but for Paul it is a religious experience.

He could have knelt down and folded his hands. There ought to have been someone to whom one could give thanks and honor—with all one's heart, and even deeper, from the very depths of one's being.

There should have been someone to whom one could pray for blessing. He saw this evening how men needed something like this—a God with whom one could communicate.[2]

On another occasion as he beholds the wonder and beauty of nature itself, he expresses his wish to worship some being who has produced this miracle and given him the feeling of humility. His cousin asks him why he cannot accept this miracle without finding it necessary to put his finger on the miracle maker. To this Paul answers:

Because I have really always thought, when I got to the top of a mountain for instance—it would be more natural to build an altar and offer some sacrifice there—rather than add a few stones to the mound. . . . If I felt like taking the butter from my tin and spreading it on the mound and making an offering to the sun—that's something that would afford me great pleasure; my religious feeling would have found some expression. If only I didn't know that I was giving the sun no pleasure in offering the butter as a sign of my gratitude. My religious feeling tells me that it is perfectly natural to worship the sun and offer it sacrifices—as long as people haven't realized that the sun is quite unconscious of us and of the good it does us.[3]

Despite her unconventional opinions Julie has been able to instill in her children a sense of moral values and personal dignity. She admonishes them to always remember the old song:

> Fight for all you hold dear,
> Die, if it must be;
> Then life will not be so hard,
> Nor death, when its time is near.[4]

She brings sunshine and fresh air into their lives and from her they learn respect for frail and tender things. At one time Paul looks at the wild orchids (*gymnadenia*) which his mother has planted in the garden. The loveliness of the tall stalks with shining wax-white flowers among the dark juniper bushes suggests something beautiful which awaits him at some time in his life. For Sigrid Undset the delicate white orchid is a symbol of earthly love and the transitoriness and uncertainty of all human life. The burning bush, on the other hand, is a symbol of the permanence of heavenly love, or of something in our lives which makes the inner soul glow with warmth and brilliance as we approach it.

Paul's first contact with Catholicism is made through the Gotaas family from whom he has rented a room while studying at the university in Oslo. These are simple devout people completely absorbed in their faith, who make no display of it before strangers. Paul is impressed by their practice of praying merely for the sake of praying and not for the sake of asking God to grant them some personal wish. Such an act of devotion gives him an insight into a new spiritual world quite different from that of enlightened thinkers who are willing to believe in any religion which answers their demands and provides a basis for their subjective religious opinions.

He attends a Catholic church service for the first time. His initial impression of the church's splendor proves to be misleading, and there is much in the service which is incomprehensible to him. Nevertheless, there is something about it all which affects him sympathetically. He feels that the priest and the congregation are all gathered together to worship some invisible being. He thinks:

> This divine service could not possibly have any other meaning. The priest did not turn to the congregation and concern himself with them; it was rather as though this man took the lead in conducting some worship or other. And for the first time in his life he thought he could perceive some meaning in divine service—in this silent adoration he could imagine that a Being was present to receive their souls.[5]

Paul has a mind as logical and clear as that of Sigrid Undset herself. He seeks a purpose in life which goes beyond comfort and self-interest, and he is therefore not interested in all the current talk about the new morality, the materialistic trend of modern civilization, or the abolition of religion. In the laws of the Church he finds something which corresponds to the needs of his moral nature: a positive attitude to eternal values and the longing of the human soul to find its origin in God. If he can only believe in a personal God and man's eternal destiny in a God-created world, then he can believe in the whole doctrine of the Church as a revealed religion based on reason. This requires a faith greater than knowledge, but if one does not have this faith, then there can be no meaning to life in the first place. With this faith, on the other hand, "the whole of life was inconceivably more wonderful and dangerous and rich, so unspeakably more serious and valuable than he had ever dreamed. He had a glimpse of paths which led out into a darkness which extended for distances greater than he could comprehend and then continued on into a light that he scarcely dared to divine." [6]

Paul falls in love with Lucy, a young shop girl, and paradoxically his relationship to her gives an even deeper meaning to his Christian experience. When Lucy becomes his mistress, he finds divine and erotic love perfectly blended. For the moment he seems to accept his mother's law of freedom of personality which sees no wrong in anything that is beautiful. However, from a priest, Father Tangen, he learns of the sacramental nature of marriage in which two people not only merge into one person, but also take upon themselves obligations and responsibilities. In Sigrid Undset's view such a sexual relationship goes beyond individual desire and carries within it the imprint of God's love for man. Father Tangen advises Paul to marry Lucy as soon as possible, for God has instituted marriage as a holy ordinance. The marriage ceremony itself would not be necessary if man were perfect, but human beings cannot be trusted by their own nature. Father Tangen explains:

Nobody can tell in advance whether a day may not come when everything within you tempts you to prove false—yes, even if you pray God to help you, you may not think He has heard, because He does not give His help in the way you yourself desire. Then it is at any rate a help to feel yourself bound by your word of honor. We men are like that. [7]

Paul plans to marry Lucy and for that reason he gives up his studies and goes into business with a friend in Trondheim. It comes as a great shock to him when he receives a letter from Lucy shortly afterwards telling him that she is breaking off their engagement. She professes her strong love for him, but feels that they would not be suited to one another in marriage. Actually Lucy feels the chasm in background and education between Paul and herself and believes that the time will surely come when Paul will feel grateful to her for leaving him. Nevertheless, Paul cannot understand how anything so beautiful could come to an end and thinks that it is without reason or justification that God has extinguished the little flame of what seemed to him a divine love.

Paul's business venture is quite successful, and a few years later he is married to a young girl named Björg Berge. How this came about was something of a riddle which even he could not comprehend. Björg is an extremely self-centered and superficial creature, hardly an ideal mate for Paul. For her marriage to a successful businessman like Paul presents the opportunity of playing a role in the social circles to which her husband and his friends belong. She has been indulged by her mother and she expects the same indulgence from Paul. Every word that falls from her mother's lips she accepts as infallible, whereas she has nothing but scorn for her father, whom she does not regard as a "fine gentleman." The religious instruction which Paul gives to their two children, Synne and Helge, is a source of irritation to Björg. However, Paul believes that he should not only teach his children to believe in God, but that he would be doing wrong to do otherwise. Nothing in the world that he might give his children or do for them would have the slightest meaning if they were to grow up without knowing God. As he holds his little daughter in his arms, he acknowledges for the first time in the presence of another person that God is the beginning and the end of all creation. He thinks:

The question therefore was not one he had always asked himself before —do you really dare to say, if you are to be honest with yourself: "I believe in one God, Father, Son, and Holy Ghost—the one the Church proclaimed nearly 2,000 years ago." The question was: Do you dare to take your own child in your arms and say: "I do not believe." [8]

Paul receives further religious instruction from Father Tangen and is then received into the Catholic Church. Here he finds the "legitimate authority" which he has always sought and which corresponds to his intuition of it. When he now enters the church and asks: "God, are You there?" he realizes that there can be no absolute authority other than that of the author himself—*Jesu, auctor vitae*, as he is called in the Litany. He looks upon Christ as the guarantor of the reality of the spiritual world.

It had been, as when, one fine day, a new light falls upon an old picture on the wall. Suddenly one discovers that there is a unity in it—the two

or three details which were all one had noticed in it before fall into
their places as parts of a composition. Things that had happened to
him, and thoughts he had years before rose up in his memory and were
given a meaning in a new context. It was just the same as with the
poems he had had to learn by heart at school—he had not even tried
to understand anything in them at that time, for, good grief, they were
only exercises to be memorized. But it sometimes happened, when such
a poem came to mind after he had grown up, that it came back illuminated by a whole chain of meaning and containing a wealth of unutter-
able thoughts.[9]

Paul's business flourishes during the boom years of World War
I (1914–1918). He is forced to be away from home for longer
periods of time, and Björg finds satisfaction in association with
people whose flattery appeals to her sense of vanity. Paul recognizes his own error in his treatment of Björg. He married her
when she was an innocent young girl and has tried to grant her
every wish, but she has been able to find pleasure only in superficial things. He has concerned himself with her physical and economic needs, but has never given any thought to her spiritual welfare even though he has been married to her for eight years.

Björg leaves Paul and her two children, becomes involved in a
love affair and finally returns home disillusioned, if not exactly
repentant. Paul is urged by his mother and cousin Ruth to divorce
his wife, who has behaved so shamelessly, but Paul takes Björg
back even though she is to have another man's child, for he feels
that through the sacrament of marriage he has bound himself to
her for life. It is not only for the sake of the children that he will
remain loyal to Björg, but also because he knows that he has
neither the right nor the desire to pass judgment on a human soul
created by God. It is Paul's temperament to enjoy religious experience. For this reason he can undergo this trial without any great
struggle or confusion, for the doctrine of the Church is more powerful than his incompatibility with Björg. Sigrid Undset's propaganda on behalf of the Catholic Church is stressed to such an
extent that all inner struggle on Paul's part is glossed over. He
goes directly to the Church and is happy to be bound by its discipline. For the same reason Paul can resist Lucy when she reappears in his life and wishes to become his mistress again. Paul's
love for Lucy is genuine and strong, but less strong than the grace

of God and the free will of the Catholic. It is easy for Paul, there-fore, in his religious ecstasy to practice self-denial.

There is a touch of the melodramatic to the conclusion of *The Burning Bush*. Lucy is brutally attacked by her estranged hus-band, who is then killed as he falls down a flight of stairs. Paul, who has come to defend Lucy, is charged with murder and im-prisoned, but later found innocent and released. Even when he is in jail, Paul is unable to harbor any ill will toward Lucy's hus-band. The man did great wrong, to be sure, but he did it in the belief that Paul was his wife's lover.

A spark of divine love seems to have become lodged in Paul as he grows in his faith and becomes more and more tolerant of all human behavior. Indeed, in practicing such patience he seems to be almost too perfect as a human being and one gets the impres-sion that Sigrid Undset has made Paul a mouthpiece of her own religious beliefs. A. H. Winsnes observes that Paul Selmer is not a representative of the Augustinian type of Christianity (like Brother Edvin in *Kristin Lavransdatter*), but of a type which Étienne Gilson calls Thomistic—from the doctrine which teaches that man's nature needs the Christian faith as a guarantee for its full development.[10] Father Tangen likewise refers to this "pure na-ture" when he tells Paul:

Perhaps you know what we Christians believe,—that once, in the be-ginning of time, there was a catastrophe, the Fall of Man. Our very nature was given a wrench—we call it original sin—and ever since it has been in utter confusion. Nothing makes our desires and passions or any part of our nature sinful, except that all the elements in it are flung helter-skelter together, so that everything is chaotic. And that was why God took upon Himself our nature—to reestablish order in it. . . . But then perhaps you know also that we teach that grace does not change our nature; it makes it perfect again.[11]

Paul is such a "pure nature." We can understand the fervor and humility of a young man who seeks refuge in the sure authority of the Church in order to avoid the chaos and bewilderment of a godless world. However, we also feel that the figure of Paul has lost something in realistic portrayal because of the tendentious-ness and extensive introduction of religious propaganda and psy-chology into this novel cycle. This is even more so in the case of

Paul's two children, who act and talk more like puppets than human beings of flesh and blood. This is particularly surprising, as Sigrid Undset's portrayal of children is otherwise so uniformly accurate and true to life.

Certainly *The Burning Bush* tends to be tedious at times because of undue space devoted to the explanation of Catholic doctrines. However, from the purely human standpoint, the novel holds the reader's interest from beginning to end because the focus, as always in Sigrid Undset's works, is not only on ideas, but also on people. Not all of them, like Paul Selmer, are interested in the search for the absolute, but all are caught up in the many tensions and real problems of everyday life. N. Elizabeth Monroe has observed that Sigrid Undset's stories always move on two levels.[12] Because of the author's profound religious experience she wishes to write of the "unbending realism" of Christianity and the rediscovery of the eternal. At the same time she realizes that most men and women never lose their contact with the commonplace and react to the problems confronting them in a practical manner and usually without any spiritual motivation. As a realistic writer Sigrid Undset is able to generate a flow of narrative at this lower level and to introduce characters whose thinking and actions conform to such commonplace circumstances. At the higher level Paul may be a mouthpiece of her religious propaganda, as mentioned above, but at the lower level he is a clearly defined young man whose life finds a new direction through his love for Lucy. Lucy herself has been described as "one of the loveliest portraits in Norwegian literature." [13]

All the other characters in the two novels are likewise drawn directly from life and described with all their virtues and faults. With a technique characteristic of saga writing Sigrid Undset is able to depict with a few bold strokes of her pen characters such as Paul's brother-in-law, the liberal theologian Halstein Garnaas, his stepmother Lillian, portrayed as the boarding-house landlady type, the intellectual convert Randi Alme, and dozens of others.

However, *The Wild Orchid* and *The Burning Bush* are primarily concerned with Paul Selmer's conversion to Catholicism, and by contrast, his mother's steadfast refusal or inability to accept her son's Christian faith. Julie Selmer, like Sigrid Undset in her youth, does not believe in God. When Paul's younger sister Tua dies, Julie turns to spiritualism in the belief that she will be reunited with her daughter in another life after death. Julie has always preferred to believe whatever was in agreement with her own desires, and for her eternal life means eternal bliss and a continuation of all the good experienced in this mortal life. Paul, however, thinks otherwise. He explains to his mother:

This material world is indeed something that God has created, but it was never meant to satisfy all our needs. I believe it is better in God's eyes that we find pleasure in this world, but more than one such mortal life is more than we can stand.[14]

Altered times and conditions make Julie disavow her optimistic faith in humanity, and in her old age she gives up her dabbling with spiritualism. There is something sad about this courageous and proud woman who is reconciled to the thought that death brings with it a dissolution into nothing. For Paul, on the other hand, the Christian view of man's eternal destiny is revealed in the church service on Good Friday. In the Cross he sees a symbol not only of man's revolt against God's will, but also of the salvation of the human soul made possible through the death and resurrection of Jesus Christ.

II Ida Elisabeth

Sigrid Undset's next novel, *Ida Elisabeth* (1932), is a realistic treatment of the problem of marriage. Although she firmly believed in the Christian concept of marriage, which has its premises in the realities of both the spiritual world and everyday life, she makes only the slightest reference to religion in this work. The novel is rather a study of the emotional drama which a woman experiences in her unhappy marriage to an irresponsible ne'er-do-well. Despite all difficulties encountered in the marriage she remains steadfast in her loyalty and is prepared to make every sacrifice to insure the welfare and happiness of her children.

In contrast to Paul Selmer, Ida Elisabeth receives no training in moral values in her home. She is left to shift for herself, for neither her father, a sailor given to drink, nor her mother gives any thought to their daughter's upbringing or education. As a schoolgirl Ida Elisabeth allows herself to be seduced by Frithjof Braatö. She is drawn to Frithjof not because of love but in a spirit of revolt against her parents and the unpleasant atmosphere in her home. She finds no pleasure in the affair with Frithjof; it seems like nothing more than a dangerous and forbidden game they are playing. Indeed, nowhere in Sigrid Undset's works do people ever find any pleasure or satisfaction in clandestine love.

When her father learns of Ida Elisabeth's misbehavior with Frithjof, he becomes furious with rage and threatens to kill her. He feels that she has been disgraced and shamed and that he has lost the only thing of beauty and purity which he has ever known in this world. He gives Frithjof a sound thrashing and then has him sent out of town. Ida Elisabeth herself leaves school and goes to work, but she likes none of her various office jobs as much as the dressmaking which she takes up in evening school.

Several years later Frithjof returns and asks Ida Elisabeth to marry him. He is well dressed, has a fairly good job, and in general seems more mature than the young boy Ida Elisabeth knew earlier. She is all the more willing to marry him because she wants to prove to herself and to the whole world that it was real love and no mere adolescent lapse which had brought them together in the first place. She is soon to learn, however, that Frithjof and all the members of the Braatö family are a hapless lot. They live upon lofty illusions and everlasting optimism, but lack all sense of discipline and are content to look to others for help in any difficulty. In their sole concern for their own welfare they remind Ida Elisabeth of a litter of young kittens that rush up when anyone has something to give them, but never learn to do anything for anyone else.

Worst of all, Frithjof has an infantile mentality, which seems to be characteristic of all the Braatö family, and a childlike incapacity to support even himself, much less a wife and family. Ida Elisabeth is a resolute and unsentimental woman who has learned to depend on her own resourcefulness and is now determined to make the best of a bad situation. Deep in her heart she knows that her father really loved her even though he often treated her badly. She feels that she has failed him and that she was responsible for the grief which brought about his early death.

Ida Elisabeth supports her husband and two children with her earnings from a small dressmaking shop. Frithjof is unable to hold any jobs, even those involving unskilled labor, and depends on Ida Elisabeth like a baby. He is content to play with the children and is responsible to a certain extent for the accidental death of

Sölvi, their older child. It annoys Ida Elisabeth to have Frithjof always around the house doing nothing. She tries to encourage him to work but is unable to arouse him from his apathy. She thinks to herself:

A mother can be both father and mother to her children, and a man can likewise be both mother and father, if misfortune takes away the mother and he is left to take care of the children. But a mother who takes the place of a father and a father in the role of a mother—no, that is just too much.[15]

A friend, Dr. Sommervold, who is acquainted with the Braatös, encourages Ida Elisabeth to divorce Frithjof, because he understands the parasitical nature of the family and thinks it is wrong that she should wear herself out in order to support a grown-up boy who belongs to other people. Ida Elisabeth has no false illusions about her marriage. She knows that Frithjof is hopelessly stupid and unreliable. On the other hand, she also knows that there are many married women whose lot is much worse than her own. It is not in her nature to discard Frithjof merely because he is a hapless creature who cannot fend for himself. But when she learns of his affair with another woman, she is determined to make an end of her unfortunate marriage. She says:

If the devil is riding on your back, you can't do anything but continue to carry him. But if the devil is obliging enough to jump off of his own free will, you can hardly imagine that anyone would be stupid enough to stoop down right away and ask him to jump on again, please.[16]

Ida Elisabeth moves to a small fjord village in the eastern part of the country. There she starts a dressmaking business and begins life anew with her two children, Carl and little Tryggve, who was born after she had left Frithjof. Formerly she always clutched at every happy moment, knowing that it would inevitably be followed by disappointment, but now she is able to enjoy life in a more relaxed manner. She devotes more time to her children, and her enthusiasm and high spirits have a salutary effect on their happiness and well-being.

Her even disposition wins her many friends, among them a fine, levelheaded lawyer, Tryggve Toksvold, who soon falls in love with her. Ida Elisabeth returns this love, for it brings her a happiness such as she has never known before, and with it she discovers a new feeling of confidence in life itself. "She had never seriously believed that there could be any happiness which simply radiated from one person to another—they didn't have to do anything more than just be together." [17]

From the beginning of their friendship it is certain that it is only a question of time before they will be married. Ida Elisabeth is happy that her two children are so small that they will have no difficulty in getting used to Tryggve as their stepfather. Suddenly, however, what shortly before appeared as a certainty, now becomes an impossibility. Else, Frithjof's sister, whom Ida Elisabeth had befriended once before by taking her into her home, reappears, this time with a child. Tryggve is displeased that Ida Elisabeth should again take up with a member of this family which has given her nothing but trouble. It is good neither for her nor her children that she should be saddled with this extra burden. He remarks: "We have an old saying in my part of the country to the effect: When misfortune's abroad it's wise to remain indoors." [18] He would not object to giving aid when necessary, but he distinguishes between those people who move under their own power like motor cars and those who are born to be trailers and always depend on others to pull them through life. He suggests that Ida Elisabeth give Else some money and send her away and also make it clear to her that she does not consider her divorced husband's kin as part of her family. Ida Elisabeth knows that Tryggve is right, but to refuse a helping hand when someone is in distress is more than she can do.

As soon as the other Braatös learn of Ida Elisabeth's whereabouts, they too reappear on the scene. Frithjof is now ill and is brought to a tuberculosis sanatorium near Ida Elisabeth's home. It is again she who must pay for this hospitalization, because there is no one else who can do it. Frithjof's parents interpret this gesture as an indication that she has forgiven him his liaison with another woman and they assume that she will take him back as soon as he is cured. Ida Elisabeth is most unhappy at this turn of events, but she reasons that Frithjof was once her husband, and even divorce cannot annul the responsibilities she assumed in marrying him. They had nothing in common except the children, and one of them Frithjof has never even seen. Nevertheless, her moral conscience prevents her from condemning anyone merely because he is different from others. She has always been annoyed whenever her mother-in-law spoke of an all-loving father, because it was all part of the Braatö jargon. Now she begins to think that, if there is a God, then there must be some meaning even in a life as feeble as Frithjof's, and God alone can understand what to others must seem so meaningless.

The greatest obstacle to Ida Elisabeth's marriage to Tryggve, however, she finds in her two children. They are jealous of the man who intervenes between their mother and themselves. Tryggve is a kindly and generous person who tries his best to win the affection of the children. He promises Ida Elisabeth that he will treat them as though they were his own and that he will raise them to be decent and respectable people. On the other hand, Tryggve tends to be somewhat stolid and easily irritated, especially when he sees inherited characteristics of the Braatö family in Ida Elisabeth's younger child and undisguised antipathy toward him in the older boy. He recognizes "the sober truth that, regardless of what he might do for the children, it would lead to nothing more than eternal dissension in his home. He might try to be a loyal friend to them, but they would repay him by disrupting his life with her, eroding their happiness and destroying their love."[19]

Ida Elisabeth, too, finds herself faced with a difficult decision. She loves Tryggve dearly, but she also has her children to think about, because they have no one to depend upon but her. The choice for her is simply whether she will follow the path of her own wishes and let her children pay the price, or renounce her own happiness, cost what it will. Ida Elisabeth chooses in favor of the children, because she does not feel free to begin a new life with Tryggve. As a mother she is inseparably bound to them and will therefore continue to devote herself to their care, just as she has in the past.

Frithjof's death does not alter the decision which the two lovers have made. It does serve, however, to pose some metaphysical and religious questions in Ida Elisabeth's mind. In the final scene of the novel Frithjof's mother consoles her dying son by reading to him some gospel passages, and his father "plays him into heaven" to the violin tune of a song which tells of the band of brave heroes who are returning after fighting the good fight down below.[20] At

first this display of sentimental religiosity seems distasteful to Ida
Elisabeth. She knows that religion for the Braatös was merely a
matter of beautiful song and poetry and emotion, and for Frithjof
it had no meaning whatsoever. Nevertheless, as Frithjof dies, Ida
Elisabeth sees a radiance and beauty in his face such as she has
never seen before. "As she stood there, she felt certain that there
existed something beyond time and space, which was just as invisible as the stars in daytime, but also just as real." [21] "Frithjof's
face itself was a kind of token that the unfathomable should not
perhaps remain so for ever." [22]

In her study *Die Ewige Frau* Gertrud von Le Fort writes of Ida
Elisabeth as the mother par excellence.[23] At the beginning of Sigrid Undset's novel Ida Elisabeth is conversing with a young
Catholic girl, Ciss Meisling, as they are returning home on the
overnight coastal steamer from Bergen. Speaking of religious
vocation, Ciss remarks: "When one sees how egotistical many
people become because of family ties and all that—then one can
understand why God selects some people to be 'everything for
everybody' just for the sake of balancing things out." [24] Ida Elisabeth who is just returning with her sick child from the doctor in
Bergen rejects this thought of renouncing her calling as mother to
her children in order to be "everything for everybody." She
thinks: "Women who have the feeling that their purpose in life is
to bear children and raise them as well as they can, hate to have
grown men come to them and oblige them to be a mother to them
too." [25]

It was for the sake of her children to whom she would give the
hope of a better future that Ida Elisabeth left her husband in the
first place. She lives only for her children and closes her heart to
her husband, his family, and indeed all who are in need of help
and compassion. However, gradually she comes to realize that a
woman cannot be a mother only to *her own* children. To be a
mother is not only to bear children but to protect and care for all
creatures. The mother must stand beside all those who are small
and weak and she must give every possible help to the irresponsible and unfortunate. Ida Elisabeth has understanding for this
broad concept of motherhood and must therefore sacrifice her
happiness with Toksvold not only because of the love of her two
sons, but because of all other children such as her husband and his
parents. A. H. Winsnes writes: "She has given her heart, and her

oblation becomes a thank-offering. Ida Elisabeth is *anima natural-iter christiana,* a soul Christian by nature." 26

III   The Faithful Wife

Sigrid Undset's next novel, *Den trofaste hustru (The Faithful Wife),* written in 1933, is again concerned with the problem of marriage and the vital role which the religious impulse plays in this human relationship. The action of the novel takes place in the mid-thirties, and the main characters are people who belong to the generation that was born in the 1890's. Many of them have a positive attitude toward a Christian faith, but others, brought up in an atmosphere of liberal thinking, look upon religion merely as a traditional relic. This latter group now finds out that the radical social and sexual ideas in which they have believed are not working. Like Julie Selmer in *The Wild Orchid* and *The Burning Bush* they have been betrayed by their optimistic faith in the infallibility of the "historical process" and the free development of personality. Their lives have become barren and insecure, because they are unable to recognize the existence of anything greater than themselves as a measure of all things.

Nathalie, who has been married to Sigurd for sixteen years, comes from such a liberal family background. Her father, the editor of a radical newspaper, was critical of pastors and the Lutheran State church. "To be sure, he had supported the liberal theologians—but merely because he thought that anything that was called liberal and progressive must necessarily belong to his party." 27

Her mother was an emancipated woman who always stood in the forefront of any struggle for a liberal cause. Ragna, Nathalie's sister, recalls that their mother was so occupied with her many women's meetings that "one would think she had found her children by accident in the wastepaper basket after a committee meeting." 28 She was just as opposed to the State church as her husband, but "she believed in the historical Jesus, because she maintained that he had been one of the pioneers in the women's rights movement, whereas the pastors and the church had never done anything but keep women in subjection." 29

Nathalie's parents were happy in the belief that they were marching forward together toward some high and noble goals, but it was not clear just what these goals were or how they were to be reached. It was necessary in any case, they thought, to break down authority in order to prepare a better future for the next generation. It turned out, however, that the new generation was so hungry for authority that they would willingly swear loyalty to the devil himself, only because his personality was undoubtedly that of a great leader.

Sigurd, Nathalie's husband, comes from a farming family in Österdal. He has a fund of common sense and like the conservative people from his part of the country distinguishes between what he knows and what he merely suspects. To do otherwise is to be guilty of the same wishful thinking that he criticizes in his parents-in-law. He says: "Any reasonable person can understand that there must be factors in operation which no one can recognize at the moment. Whether anyone will be lucky enough to discover them later on, we cannot say. For the present, we can do no more than recognize their existence." [30]

In contrast to other married couples in Sigrid Undset's novels Sigurd and Nathalie are economically well situated. They both have their professions, he as an engineer and she in an important administrative position in a textile business. Except for a purely physical relationship, they have little in common. Neither is interested in the work, hobbies, or friends of the other. They have separate rooms at home and even take their vacations at different times. Nevertheless, they have enjoyed a supposedly happy married life for sixteen years. During the first years of their marriage Nathalie was obliged to work in order to help Sigurd through some difficult times. Later she continued to work, even when it was no longer necessary from the financial standpoint. They have no children and all Nathalie's love is therefore centered in Sigurd. For her the most sacred thing in life is her love for her husband. She tells her sister Gerda: "What I lacked as a child and a young girl I found when I became acquainted with Sigurd. I don't believe that any religion could have satisfied that need. And after I married Sigurd, I no longer felt that I lacked anything. . . . I have often thought that I have had my share of happiness and no one can ask for more than that." [31] Gerda recognizes the truth when she answers: "I guessed as much, all the time in Oslo. For you, love was a surrogate for religion." [32]

Nathalie is intellectually superior to Sigurd and he has evidently developed a sense of inferiority because he is aware of this fact. One suspects that he has not found the same fulfillment in marriage as Nathalie. He reveals his own narcissism when he confesses: "It wasn't only you I loved; to a certain extent I was also in love with myself, that is, in the image of myself which you had created." [33]

The marriage may have brought satisfaction and happiness to Nathalie, but with the passing of years it has brought only boredom and ennui to Sigurd. He feels that Nathalie and he have not pulled together in their marriage. She has been a good and loyal wife, but because he has had to accept her help and support, it has become clear to him that she is the more successful, intelligent, and energetic of the two. Perhaps it is also an indication of Nathalie's egotism that in her feeling of profound security she is the last to recognize the signs of estrangement in their marital life.

It comes as a great shock to Nathalie when she learns that Sigurd has deceived her with Adinda Gaarder, a young Catholic girl who is to bear his child. Adinda will not marry Sigurd nor will she let the child be taken from her. She loves Sigurd, but as a devout Catholic she realizes that she has become involved in an affair which is in conflict with her religious convictions and she is prepared to take the consequences. Nathalie feels that she has been put to shame and rejected by Sigurd and sees the cause of all their difficulties in the fact that they have had no children. She concludes that no matter how much two people can give to each other in a love relationship, there is always an inner voice which tells one that real personal fulfillment lies in having children.

After her separation from Sigurd, Nathalie becomes the mistress of Sverre, a friend of her childhood. She does not love Sverre, but is drawn to him because in her loneliness she feels the need of someone to protect her. She soon breaks with him, however, and then with the death of Adinda in childbirth the stage is set for her reconciliation with Sigurd. Nathalie would wish that they resume their life just as it was before, but Sigurd, who has always had some religious faith, wishes to reestablish their union on a completely new basis. He explains to her that their marriage failed because it did not have its foundation in God. He says to Nathalie: "You have never pretended to believe in God. You can understand that I consider it quite natural that our marriage should have ended as badly as it did." [34] He speaks of essential realities which surround us and which cannot be ignored. Nathalie asks him if his religion is not merely a matter of wishful thinking and he answers: "If you'll be honest, Nathalie—don't you think that many of the people you have known, who say they don't believe in God, in fact *wish* that He existed? Existed as a reality which, like a hand, grasps everything—and nothing we desire or imagine can help us to slip out between his fingers?"[35]

Nathalie has never felt this longing for God nor does she have any understanding for the spiritual values of Sigurd's faith. On numerous occasions she renounces all belief in the supernatural and a life after death. Her love for Sigurd is the only thing which has meaning for her, but now that he has been returned to her, she does acknowledge that it must be "wonderful to have someone to thank."[36] She can understand what Sigurd's faith must mean to him, but she cannot accept it without warping her own personality. Nevertheless, Nathalie can be loyal to her own beliefs. Sigurd says to her:

By *nature* you are more religious than any of us. . . . You are much more willing to be as you think you should be, and do what you think you ought to do, whether you want to or not. . . . You are in fact more loyal to that which you have been taught to believe than most Christians are to God. And that, even though you constantly criticized those who taught you, but who had so little confidence in what they were preaching. I think that's real piety.[37]

In spite of such loyalty it is difficult to understand just how Nathalie and Sigurd are able to solve their marital tangle. To be sure, they now no longer have a childless marriage, for Nathalie adopts the child of a co-worker who has died and Sigurd has the responsibility of raising his and Adinda's child. However, it was not the childless marriage, but the lack of some common ideal, which had disrupted the marriage in the first place. It would seem that nothing has been changed in this respect. One may anticipate that Sigurd like Paul Selmer will instruct his child in the teachings of the Christian faith, whereas Nathalie will raise her adopted child in a manner of which Sigurd will undoubtedly disapprove. Sigurd's concept of a Christian marriage and of life itself as a preparation for eternity is very much in agreement with Sigrid Undset's own viewpoint, but Nathalie makes very little attempt to view life except in its direct relationship to her own personal happiness. Her mother may have had some liberal ideas which did not appeal to Nathalie, but she also had some good moral teachings which she might well have heeded. Her mother once said: "There is so much else in this world to live for. There are so many people one can help and do something for. He who lives to serve others and to make them happy, will never have time to be unhappy."[38] Nathalie, however, speaks of her longing for an intimate and warm place where Sigurd and she may find happiness, but from which all others are excluded.

The Faithful Wife is a realistic novel of married life. It is a penetrating study based on the author's familiarity with the science of psychology. The story is told with intensity and detachment and at no time does it become didactic or argumentative. The two main characters are clearly defined and the motivation is artistically correct. Nevertheless, the novel must be considered one of Sigrid Undset's weaker efforts, chiefly because the reader misses any development in Nathalie's thinking. The factors which brought about the marital rift are still present at the end. Nathalie reveals no tendency or willingness to accept any religious faith, even though Sigurd maintains that it is impossible for people to live and work together unless they believe in God. The author seems to leave the reader with the impression that Nathalie and Sigurd have been happily reunited, but it is difficult to understand how there can be any permanency in this union. Sigurd, to be sure, recognizes the primacy of the spiritual in the marital relationship, but Nathalie sees in it merely a satisfying sexual experience which has no relevancy to the social or spiritual scheme of the world. There are many women in Sigrid Undset's novels who think like Nathalie, but no other woman who fails to see the life of the senses as part of a divine plan finds happiness in marriage. It is for this reason that the conclusion of *The Faithful Wife* leaves the reader somewhat bewildered.

IV Madame Dorthea

Madame Dorthea (1939) is a historical novel written at Lillehammer just before the invasion of Norway by the Nazi troops in the spring of 1940. The novel was never completed because of the fury of the war which forced Sigrid Undset to flee from her homeland and seek refuge in the United States. As a homeless exile, whose eldest son had died a soldier's death defending his country against the invader, she was now no longer interested in writing fiction. While she was in the United States, Sigrid Undset was actively involved in waging a war of words against Nazis, Fascists, and Communists and their anti-Christian ideologies, in which she saw a threat to the existence of the free world.

In this historical novel Sigrid Undset does not write of the Middle Ages, but of the Age of Enlightenment in the eighteenth century when people looked upon the Middle Ages as a period of ignorance and superstition from which they were now liberated through the God-given "light of reason."

Concerning the sources of *Madame Dorthea* A. H. Winsnes writes: "On her mother's side, the family tradition provided a living and unbroken connection with the eighteenth century. Living contacts with that age were her mother and, perhaps even more, her grand-aunt ("Moster"), who was born in 1814 and died in 1905, mentally alert and lively to the end. Moster told legends and fairy-tales which had come from her father, Dean Vilhelm Adolf Worsöe, and he had them from his Norwegian home, the glass-factory of Nöstetangen, where his father had been overseer. The setting of *Madame Dorthea* is the glass-factory at Biri, but nevertheless it was the tradition from Nöstetangen which played a prominent part in the book's creation. The old stories, which had been told in the overseer's house at the glass-factory here late in the eighteenth century, were brought back to Norway by the little girl who sat and listened to Moster's tales a hundred years later. Not that *Madame Dorthea* is a repetition of Moster's stories, but they were of essential significance for the inner life of the novel." [39]

The setting of the novel is a remote East Norwegian village in the 1790's. The social and cultural background is described with authentic realism, and the characters are products of the age in which they live. In external details Sigrid Undset is able to recreate the atmosphere of a bygone era, just as she does in her medieval novels. Nevertheless, the story could be told of any time, for to her way of thinking the people are always more important than the period, and she sees the universal and timeless in all human character. Madame Dorthea and Kristin Lavransdatter are just as modern as Uni Hirsch, Rose Wagner, Ida Elisabeth, or any of the other women in Sigrid Undset's contemporary novels.

By contrast to the other novels the action of *Madame Dorthea* is limited to a short span of about six or seven months. Jörgen Thestrup, Madame Dorthea's husband and manager of the glass factory, has disappeared under mysterious circumstances while searching for their two eldest sons, Vilhelm aged fifteen and Claus aged fourteen. The young boys had driven out in a snowstorm with their tutor, the talented but untrustworthy Augustin Dabbelsteen. After many anxious hours of waiting the boys are returned home safely, but Jörgen fails to come back, nor is there any indication of what fate may have befallen him. Imagination runs riot as the common people seek some explanation for Jörgen's disappearance. Madame Dorthea thinks to herself: "How curious it was, this taste for horror stories among the common people. Their talk had concerned itself with nothing but murders and executions, witchcraft and witch burnings, ghosts, and bad omens—it was as though they were all competing to see who could tell the most terrible tale. . . . For that matter, Thestrup had admitted that he too had had some strange experiences both in the churchyard lane and near the glassworks at nighttime." [40] There is even a suggestion that Dorthea's husband may have left home and gone abroad for some unexplained reason.

During the difficult months which follow, Dorthea keeps her countenance very well. She tries to assuage her personal grief as she makes plans for the future of her seven young children. It is now that we learn that Dorthea had been married off as a young girl to an elderly pastor. In the eighteenth century a young girl could not object to the marriage plans which her parents had arranged for her, even though it meant burying herself alive as a companion and nurse to an old man. After the death of her first husband, Dorthea might very well have made another "mariage de raison." However, after she met Jörgen Thestrup she knew that "the natural, modest contentment which a woman may achieve in such a marriage of reason could no longer have satisfied her. She would have been poorly fitted to make a respectable husband . . . as happy as he deserved to be." At the side of her beloved Jörgen she had known the meaning of complete happiness. "She had come to see that love is a dangerous power. And if it had been granted to one to taste the joys of love while at the same time striving to comply with the dictates of duty and virtue, then one can never thank Providence enough for this rare mercy." [41]

The bonds between her and Jörgen were strengthened not only by the joys they had experienced together, but also by the trials and tribulations which had been placed upon them by the fatherly hand of an all-loving God.

In the disappearance of her husband Jörgen, however, Dorthea sees an indication of the inconstancy and insecurity of human life. Her faith in God seems to waver as she seeks the answer to her husband's fate from a strolling gypsy woman. Her rational mind makes a strong effort to discount the gypsy's power of second sight and she is reproved for her disbelief. The gypsy says: "If you had had faith I could have done some good to you and your family with what I have in this box. But I know well enough, you big people have little faith in the wisdom of the gypsies—it seems that you don't believe in the almighty God either or in the other man whose name I will not mention in this place." [42]

Dorthea learns nothing from the gypsy and she is annoyed with herself to think that she has sought the aid of this person.

She was not even sure whether she had done it because she really believed that this mysterious woman had some occult power, or in spite of the fact that she was convinced that the whole thing was deception and hocus-pocus. One thing was just as bad as the other.

Ah yes—in her heart she had certainly hoped that the stranger was in possession of sources of knowledge which flowed in mysterious depths to which the clear daylight of reason could not penetrate. And she who had believed she loved this blessed daylight with all her soul—no sooner did its rays seem to her cold and pitiless, because they revealed a deplorable present and an uncertain future—than she sought refuge in a superstitious hope that the wandering gypsies might after all possess such mysterious powers as the common people attributed to them. [43]

Dorthea is repulsed and frightened by the thought that she has tried to speculate about mysterious forces which lie beyond the bounds of reason. She then turns to Scharlach, the pious old foreman of the glassworks of which Thestrup was the manager. Scharlach, a Catholic living in a Protestant cultural milieu, has the same simple piety and boundless faith in God's inscrutable providence as Brother Edvin in *Kristin Lavransdatter*. Dorthea is not interested in the mystical side of the Christian religion, and it runs counter to her good sense and reason to think that through prayer all men may be cleansed from sins and be partakers in His redemption. "Scharlach, Scharlach," she says, "all that is fanaticism and the aberration of an overwrought state of mind. A dark superstition that leads to nothing, except to prevent the clear and lofty light of religion from penetrating our understanding and ennobling it." [44]

Dorthea speaks as an intelligent woman representing the rationalism of the eighteenth century. She does not wish to take Scharlach's faith from him, but she looks upon it as religious extravagance and visionary effusion and refuses to have her children infected by it. She has faith in God, but attends church only irregularly because she cannot bear to listen to the pastor's meaningless platitudes. Scharlach, on the other hand, recognizes the existence of a spiritual power beyond the visible world and man's unique position as part of a supernatural reality. He says to Dorthea: "You certainly have an intelligent mind and a kind disposition, and Manager Thestrup did too, God bless him. But it is not *enough*, Madame—that religion enlightens our reason. Reason is good to have and to use, but it is only part of our spirit—just as the day is good and blessed—but it is only part of the twenty-four hours." [45] He explains that the blessed sun and the lovely light of reason are given to us for our good, but he adds: "Nevertheless, the sun must set every evening, so that we can see how many stars there are in the heavens—each one of them a sun, and said to be just as great and beautiful as our own." [46] He does not overlook the fact that there are many people who use their day and their intelligence to torment and cheat and fleece their neighbors. He concludes: "Ah no, Madame Thestrup—we can just as easily use our intelligence for evil as for good." [47]

Madame Dorthea cannot distinguish between genuine intelligence and goodness. For her as for Julie Selmer reason is the basis for all life's orientation. She admits that she has been tempted by the mystical aspect of religion, but she rejects it emphatically as she answers Scharlach: "There may be a good deal of truth in your extravagant fanaticism, Scharlach—for fanaticism it is. And in spite of all you can say it is related to all that terrible belief in ghosts and fairies and signs and omens and all the things that human imagination associates with darkness." [48]

Because of her rationalistic mind Madame Dorthea sees a certain ambiguity in all religion and she is therefore reluctant to ac-

cept what she cannot logically understand. At the same time she is
gifted with the same natural piety which Ida Elisabeth and Nathalie possess in such rich measure. Scharlach recognizes Madame
Dorthea's abiding faith in God and for this reason he can reassure
her at the end of the novel that she will never be altogether unhappy.

Sigrid Undset has often expressed her view that there must be a
harmonious balance between the intellectual and emotional in all
religious experience. A religion steeped in emotion, but without
an intellectual foundation, can lead only to fanciful superstition.
On the other hand, pure reason alone with complete disregard for
the feelings and emotions, which are a real and genuine part of
man's inner nature, will of necessity produce a barren world.

There is very little plot in the story of Madame Dorthea, nor is
there much development of character in the figure of the heroine,
such as one expects to find in Sigrid Undset's works. Nevertheless,
events seem to be steeped in reality. Had Sigrid Undset been able
to complete the novel, it is certain that the figure of Madame Dorthea would have emerged more clearly. All of the author's fictional
heroines sooner or later become aware that there are inexplicable
currents in all human affairs, and with the exception of Jenny
Winge and Charlotte Hedels all are able to adjust to the difficulties facing them. The reader senses that Madame Dorthea too will
be able to make the necessary adjustment. Although she has been
brought up to worship the pure light of reason, she has shown,
particularly in her relationship to her husband and children, that
she is a woman whose actions and thinking are governed by her
innate kindness and the warmth of her feeling. In her concern for
the future of her children and also in her readiness to help others
less fortunate than herself she exemplifies perfectly Sigrid Undset's concept of the ideal mother. She derives the greatest satisfaction from her life's calling as mother, and for this reason one feels
certain that after these trying months she will eventually find happiness and inner peace.

As a counterbalance to the thinness of the plot the author has
introduced a large galaxy of very real minor characters. There is
the worldly and dissolute Captain Cold, a disgraced army officer
living with his housekeeper-mistress Marie Langseth, but unwilling to marry her because he does not wish to risk his chances for
reinstatement by being saddled with an unpresentable wife. Mad-

ame Dorthea recalls that the very sight of Captain Cold was always a source of irritation to Jörgen. Possibly her husband was also stirred by a feeling of jealousy to see his wife conversing with this dashing officer. Madame Dorthea, on the other hand, has a feeling of compassion for this unfortunate individual who has been the sport of a capricious fate. She refuses to condemn him because she knows that he is not completely without feeling and that his conscience must be torturing him enough for the tragedy he has brought upon Marie and himself.

One of the most colorful characters portrayed by Sigrid Undset is Elisabeth, Dorthea's robust and domineering mother, now married for the fourth time. Events in her checkered life include marriages to a major, then to David Frazer, the major's clerk, then to a wealthy clergyman, Dean de Theilemann, and finally to the young peasant-born sheriff and corporal, Haagen Lunde. A violent outburst of Elisabeth's one-time associate, the vituperative harridan, Aleth Dabbelsteen, suggests that Elisabeth may have had her first husband killed in order to be able to marry David Frazer, Dorthea's father. Elisabeth does not let herself be perturbed by such talk. When she married Haagen Lunde she is supposed to have said that "she preferred a live sheriff to a dead dean and a warm corporal in his bed to an embalmed major in a leaden coffin." [49]

As in her medieval novels, so too in this novel of the eighteenth century does Sigrid Undset introduce us to the daily round of activity in a woman's life. A description of the kitchen and of other rooms in the home, of clothing, utensils, customs, and practices all contribute to the impression of reality which the writer has tried to create. From the cultural standpoint perhaps the most interesting part of the novel is the description of the peasant wedding at Lunde when Dorthea's young half-brother, Ole Haagensen, is married to a neighboring peasant's daughter. The literary Norwegian, of which Sigrid Undset makes use, as well as the peasant dialect spoken at Lunde, the Norwegian mixed with German spoken by Scharlach and the members of his family, and a letter to Dorthea written in perfect eighteenth-century Danish likewise help to recreate the spirit and atmosphere of this bygone age.

Madame Dorthea was left uncompleted when Sigrid Undset fled Norway in the spring of 1940. The author's younger sister,

Mrs. Signe Undset Thomas, has informed me that the second part of the novel was to deal primarily with Madame Dorthea's two oldest sons who leave home after the disappearance of their father in order to fashion their own lives in the outside world. However, upon her arrival in the United States Sigrid Undset said that she no longer had any time for literature. *Madame Dorthea* lay far behind her; her sole interest now was to write in support of the war effort.

In some short articles the author does, to be sure, "return to the past," as she recalls some of her happy earlier experiences in Norway, but for the most part she lives in the present and her articles and speeches of this period reflect her concern for the fate of her country and the cause of democracy throughout the world. She speaks with the voice of her countrymen in her bitter indictment of Nazi treachery and brutality. Her expression of hate is so vehement that she forgets the artist's detachment whenever she speaks of Germany. She recalls that Norwegians and only Norwegians have lived in Norway for at least 3,000 years and they have lived at peace with the world for over a hundred years. Norwegians and indeed all Scandinavian people have a passion for justice and a love of liberty. The oldest laws of their lands proclaim: "With law shall the land be built up and never destroyed with lawlessness." [50] However, it was the mistake of free countries to think that all other people had the same longing and respect for justice as they.

She points out that the ideas of the democracies about freedom, equality, and brotherhood are the fruits of Christianity and any democracy without Christianity is a wishful dream. The Nazis, Fascists, and Communists have shown themselves to be irreconcilable foes of Christianity; totalitarian states have never understood what a precious thing personal freedom is, and they ignore the fact that man is intended for eternity.

Despite all her bitterness Sigrid Undset is nevertheless able to pray: "May God save us from denying the Germans our help." [51] For Christian and humanitarian reasons it will be necessary to neutralize our hate in the work of reconstruction after the war. The democratic way is the only guarantee of a better future as we begin "the work of rebuilding a society of free nations and free people whose duty and right it is to fight for a greater sense of responsibility of men toward one another, for justice and for more secure and happy living conditions." [52]

Sigrid Undset believed that the United States as the greatest democracy in the world would be expected to take the lead in reestablishing order and creating goodwill among the free nations after the cessation of hostilities. There is thus particular significance in the thoughts which went through her mind as her ship brought her closer and closer to America. In *Return to the Future* she writes: "It was not only in body that we came closer to our native land each day the ship carried us over the Pacific Ocean, and the train took us from California to New York. Having fled from the Nazi invasion of Norway, through Soviet Russia and Japan, I knew that coming to America was like setting out on the homeward journey. Now it is only across America that the road leads back to the future—that which we from the European democracies call future." [53]

CHAPTER 6

Conclusion

IN an address delivered in New York on May 24, 1942, Sigrid Undset spoke these words of advice to other Catholic writers: "Tell the truths you have to. Even if they are grim, preposterous, shocking. After all, we Catholics ought to acknowledge what a shocking business human life is. Our race has been revolting against its Creator since the beginning of time. Revolt, betrayal, denial, or indifference, sloth, laziness—which of us has not been guilty in one or more or all of these sins some time or other? But remember you have to tell other and more cheerful truths, too: of the Grace of God and the endeavor of strong and loyal, or weak but trusting souls, and also of the natural virtues of man created in the image of God, an image it is very hard to efface entirely." [1]

In all her works Sigrid Undset sought to reveal these objective truths without any sentimentality or romantic idealism. With her keen eye for detail and the accuracy of her background description she carries on the tradition of realistic writers of the second half of the nineteenth century. However, that which distinguishes Sigrid Undset from her predecessors in the field of the realistic novel is her constant preoccupation with the inner lives of her characters. The men and women she writes about, whether they live in the present or in the past, are all influenced by the customs and mores of their particular age, but in the final analysis it is not society but the individual himself who is responsible for his eventual success or failure. On numerous occasions she has expressed this thought in the words: "Every man is the architect of his own fate."

Sigrid Undset draws a gray and somber picture of human existence. She never closes her eyes to reality by pretending not to see the "hideous or painful or discouraging truths." [2] She describes human despair and wretchedness with intensity and brutal realism. Yet it is not a picture of unrelieved gloom, for with her positive attitude toward life she is able to find a basis for hope and optimism in man's ability to discriminate between good and evil and his willingness to subordinate his will to that of a spiritual authority. Ibsen may have found man's mind base and petty, but Sigrid Undset sees the likeness of God in man's soul. The path to redemption brings with it great suffering, but it is through suffering that man gains inner strength and becomes aware of his own worth in a divine plan.

Sigrid Undset looks deeply into the hearts and minds of her characters, and with her technique of psychological investigation has them speak for themselves and thus reveal their innermost thoughts without any intervention on her part. As a strict moralist she exalts only positive values. She cannot condone the sins and transgressions of mankind, but she is not relentless in her judgment, for she knows that all human emotions and passions, for evil as well as for good, are part of common reality and cannot be glossed over.

It is for this reason that the sexual impulse plays such a prominent part in Sigrid Undset's works. If she is daring (for her day and age) in her description of the erotic, it is because she recognizes the centrality of sex in all human existence. She is sharply critical of puritanical prudishness which she considers responsible for the hypocrisy and moral anarchy of her time. The life of the senses is nothing to be disregarded and casually swept aside. It is an ever-present reality and for this reason her important characters are all creatures of flesh and blood who live full robust lives. She is therefore resolute in her handling of sexual matters, but there is nothing in her work which stimulates lasciviousness. She recognizes love as a force of nature, but the sexual relationship can bring only barren pleasure unless it has some other end in view. Love has no rights of its own. It is bound by laws imposed from without, for it demands sacrifice and abnegation. All Sigrid Undset's heroes and heroines eventually learn that happiness is no fixed or ready-made condition. Only by transcending the narrow limits of their own personalities and by accepting the full burden of responsibility toward family and society are they able to break out of their loneliness and find happiness in the communal solidarity of human relationships.

It is characteristic of the writer's psychological realism that she portrays men and women just as they are, neither as paragons of

virtue nor scoundrels devoid of any redeeming qualities. Even the
best have their human frailties. The monks Gunnulf and Edvin
have experienced moments of consuming passion, and Lavrans
too, a model Christian in most ways, knows only too well how far
he falls short of his own ideals. On the other hand, Lady Aashild
despite her sinful past and un-Christian ways is able to win our
sympathy because of the kindness she shows Kristin at the time of
the young woman's marriage to Erlend. We are likewise drawn to
Eirik, Ingunn's illegitimate son, because we can see how he grows
in moral stature. As he comes under the influence of the Church's
teachings, he sloughs off his youthful faults and revitalizes his own
life.

The themes of Sigrid Undset's novels and essays are remarkably
limited. As a woman as well as an author she has a deeply committed social awareness. She believes in the old virtues of wisdom,
justice, truth, mercy, moderation, and above all loyalty and a
sense of responsibility. Loyalty is reflected first of all in man's relationship to the family unit, the pivot of society, for Sigrid Undset
believes in the sanctity of marriage and the inviolability of the
home. As she sees it, most men and women look upon loyalty as
the most precious possession they have; others with their restless
hearts are incapable of loyalty and are forced to suffer the tragic
fate of isolation and loneliness in a godless world. A. H. Winsnes
writes: "It is the capacity for loyalty in men and women which is
put to the test. The conflict of conscience which results from disloyalty—the conscience tormented with the conscience saved—is
the theme which constantly recurs. For this reason, her writing
revolves around the central relationships in life in which loyalty is
demanded, whether a pact must be kept or service rendered—between husband and wife, parents and children, the individual and
his home, family and country." [3]

As a deep religious faith was added to her moral idealism and
ethical convictions Sigrid Undset raised this concept of loyalty
into a higher sphere. With Christianity a new significance was
given to man's position in a supernatural world of the spirit. God
is the one unchanged reality and through His redemptive grace
every human being, great or small, chieftain or serf, shares in His
eternal kingdom. It is a basic tenet of the Christian faith that man
has his origin in God and is called to be His servant on earth. All
his actions are of cosmic significance, for he is responsible not only

to family and social order but also to God with whom he is joined in a covenant. A violation of his code of honor is a wrong against society, but beyond that it is also a sin in the face of God. Often a conflict arises in man's mind between the longing to do God's will and the desire to follow his self-will. In *Olav Audunssön* Sigrid Undset tells of the battle that has been waged in the universe since the beginning of time between God and His enemies.[4] Every human being must take part in this struggle on one side or the other, for man has been given the free will to choose between loyalty and disloyalty and must therefore serve God or break the pact made with Him.

Such is the nature of the dramatic struggle waged by Olav Audunssön and Kristin Lavransdatter. Both are proud protagonists who may not always have lived in the light, but who nevertheless have never repudiated life. It takes them both a lifetime of struggle and suffering before they learn how to find satisfaction in accepting the full burden of their responsibilities and it is only at the very threshold of death itself that they finally submit in self-surrender to a spiritual authority. Every aspect of their lives is brought into harmony with their religious development, for to the medieval mind everything in the world was ultimately dependent on God.

Sigrid Undset as a devout Christian knows that religion can never become outmoded. The plight of modern man is no different from that of medieval man six hundred years ago, and the message of the Church has as much relevance today as it did then. The heroes and heroines of her contemporary novels are forced to wage the same battle as Kristin and Olav, even though not in such a dramatic or psychologically penetrating way. Sooner or later, however, they all become aware of the tragedy of their lives when divorced from all reality. They find no happiness until they are able to free themselves from the narrow confines of their own personality and embrace a life of responsibility. Sigrid Undset believes that nothing in life escapes connection with the eternal. In the story of her conversion to Catholicism she writes: "Already in this life on earth we can experience so much contact with the divine that we know life can be happiness. And it shall remain so even if we were to live until eternity as long as we constantly renew our strength from that spiritual power which is the source of everything on earth." [5]

   As a realistic writer Sigrid Undset expresses most clearly her
affirmation of life, but as a Christian she never loses sight of the
fact that man's ultimate purpose is to find the proper relationship
to his Creator.

Notes and References

Chapter One

1. *Elleve aar*, p. 17.
2. *Ibid.*, p. 76.
3. *Ibid.*, p. 330.
4. At the beginning of the manuscript of *Husfrue* Sigrid Undset wrote: "In memory of my father Ingvald Undset."
5. *Elleve aar*, pp. 138, 306.
6. *Ibid.*, p. 285.
7. *Ibid.*, p. 271.
8. *Ibid.*, pp. 261, 317.
9. "Strömmen tyner," in Rikard Berge, *Norsk sogukunst* (Oslo, 1924), p. 140.
10. *Elleve aar*, pp. 176–77.
11. *Ibid.*, p. 265.
12. *Ibid.*, p. 289.
13. *Ibid.*, p. 338.
14. *Ibid.*, p. 288.
15. *Ibid.*, p. 287.
16. "Florida Water," in *Artikler og taler fra krigstiden*, ed. by A. H. Winsnes (Oslo, 1952), p. 40.
17. *Urd*, May 28, 1910.
18. "Om Sigrid Undsets barndomshjem og tidlige ungdom," in *Samtiden* (Oslo, 1958), pp. 39–46.
19. A. H. Winsnes, *Sigrid Undset. En Studie i kristen realisme* (Oslo, 1949). Translated by P. G. Foote, *Sigrid Undset. A Study in Christian Realism* (London, 1953), p. 34.
20. *Elleve aar*, pp. 304–305. Cf. also "En bok som blev et vendepunkt i mitt liv," in Winsnes, ed., *Artikler og taler*, pp. 27–34.
21. "Pinse i Rom," in *Morgenbladet* (Oslo, June, 1910, No. 308).
22. Nini Roll Anker, *Min venn Sigrid Undset* (Oslo, 1946).
23. *Ibid.*, p. 12.
24. *Ibid.*, p. 13.
25. *Ibid.*, pp. 28–29.

26. *Et kvindesynspunkt* (Oslo, 1919). The volume includes the following articles: "Nogen kvindesaksbetragtninger," 1912 ("Some Observations on the Suffragette Movement"); "Det fjerde bud," 1914 ("The Fourth Commandment"); "Kvinderne og verdenskrigen," 1918 ("Women and the World War"); "Begrepsforvirring," 1919 ("Confusion of Ideas") and "Efterskrift," 1919 ("Postscript").

27. *Ibid.,* p. 161.

28. Anker, *op. cit.,* p. 32.

29. *Ibid.,* pp. 33–34.

30. Winsnes, *Sigrid Undset,* p. 78.

31. Signe Undset Thomas in the introduction to Sigrid Undset's *Lykkelige dager* (Oslo, 1960), p. 5. The Danes liked to think that the Norwegians were very chauvinistic. Bjerkebæk, a character in an old Danish comedy, represented this type of Norwegian braggart.

32. Anker, *op. cit.,* p. 65.

33. Edvard Bull, *Folk og kirke i middelalderen* (Oslo, 1912), p. 15.

34. Fredrik Paasche, "Sigrid Undset og norsk middelalder," in *Samtiden* (Oslo, 1929), pp. 1–12.

35. In *Edda* (Oslo, 1921), pp. 1–39.

36. *Tre sagaer om islændinger* (Oslo, 1923). Volume includes *Viga-Glums-saga, Kormaks-saga,* and *Bandamanna-saga.*

37. Published together with *Fortellingen om Viga-Ljot og Vigdis* in Vol. X of Sigrid Undset's medieval novels.

38. Included in *Saga of Saints,* translated by E. C. Ramsden (New York, 1934), pp. 87–148.

39. "Klosterliv" ("Monastery Life"), "Paa pilegrimsferd" ("On Pilgrim's Path"), and "Sognekirken" ("The Parish Church") in *Norsk kulturhistorie,* ed. by A. Bugge and Sverre Steen (Oslo, 1939), Vol. II, 300–52, 353–84, 385–432.

40. Anker, *op. cit.,* p. 57.

41. Victor Vinde, *Sigrid Undset: A Nordic Moralist.* Translated from the French into English by Babette and Glenn Hughes (Seattle, 1930), p. 25.

42. Included in Haakon Bergwitz' *De sökte de gamle stier* (Oslo, 1936), pp. 83–96.

43. *Kristin Lavransdatter. Kransen,* Med. I, 38.

44. *Kristin Lavransdatter. Husfrue,* Med. III, 127–34.

45. Carl F. Engelstad, *Mennesker og makter: Sigrid Undsets middelalderromaner* (Oslo, 1940), p. 36.

46. "Förste kveld paa Montecassino" in *Det kimer i klokker* (Oslo, 1925). Quoted by Winsnes, *Sigrid Undset,* p. 90.

47. *Katolsk propaganda* (Oslo, 1927).

48. "Sommer paa Gotland," in *Selvportretter og landskapsbilleder,* p. 204.

Notes and References 163

49. "Brev til en sogneprest," in *Etapper. Ny række*, p. 207.
50. "Den sterkeste magt," in *Selvportretter og landskapsbilleder*, p. 163.
51. *Gymnadenia*, Mod. VI, 116.
52. "Blasfemi," in *Selvportretter og landskapsbilleder*, p. 21.
53. *Ibid.*, p. 30.
54. "Brev til en sogneprest," p. 220.
55. *De sökte de gamle stier*, p. 94.
56. "Brev til en sogneprest," p. 211.
57. *Begegnungen und Trennungen* (Munich, 1931), p. 13.
58. Included in Winsnes, ed., *Artikler og taler*, p. 269.
59. *Tilbake til fremtiden*, p. 10. Cf. also Winsnes, *Sigrid Undset*, p. 220.
60. *Tilbake til fremtiden*, pp. 29, 39, and passim.
61. *Ibid.*, p. 62.
62. *Ibid.*, pp. 72–171.
63. *Ibid.*, p. 117.
64. *Ibid.*, p. 127.
65. Arne Skouen, "Sigrid Undset i Amerika," in *Samtiden* (Oslo, 1947). Cf. also *New York Times*, April 26, 1940.
66. "Skjönne Amerika," in Winsnes, ed., *Artikler og taler*, pp. 199–206.
67. "Min gate," in Winsnes, ed., *Artikler og taler*, pp. 195–98.
68. "Amerikansk litteratur" in Winsnes, ed., *Artikler og taler*, pp. 207–13.
69. "Arven vaar fra Sola," in Winsnes, ed., *Artikler og taler*, pp. 270–74. Cf. also *New York Times*, December 6, 1942.
70. *New York Times*, April 23, 1940.
71. *Tilbake til fremtiden*, p. 178.
72. "Kristendom og humanisme," in Winsnes, ed., *Artikler og taler*, p. 300.
73. "Kristen kultur," in Winsnes, ed., *Artikler og taler*, p. 310.
74. N. Elizabeth Monroe, *The Novel and Society* (Chapel Hill, 1941), p. 40.
75. "Brorskapets religion," in Winsnes, ed., *Artikler og taler*, p. 322.
76. In introduction to *Twelve Stories by Steen Steensen Blicher* (New York, 1945), p. 21.
77. Later translated into Norwegian as *Sigurd og hans tapre venner* (Oslo, 1955).
78. Included in Winsnes, ed., *Artikler og taler*, pp. 171–92.
79. *Ibid.*, pp. 189–90.
80. Cf. Arne Skouen, *op. cit.*
81. A. H. Winsnes, *Sigrid Undset: Artikler og taler fra krigstiden* (Oslo, 1952).

82. *New York Times,* May 21, 1943.
83. In University Library, Oslo.

Chapter Two

1. *Fru Marta Oulie,* Mod. I, 20–21.
2. *Ibid.,* p. 20.
3. *Ibid.,* p. 52.
4. *Ibid.,* p. 28.
5. *Ibid.,* p. 9.
6. *Ibid.,* p. 66.
7. *En fremmed,* Mod. I, 100.
8. *Ibid.,* p. 176.
9. *Den lykkelige alder,* Mod. I, 212–13.
10. *Ungdom* (Oslo, 1910).
11. *Den lykkelige alder,* p. 214.
12. *Ibid.,* p. 228.
13. *Ibid.,* p. 257.
14. *Elleve aar,* pp. 304–305.
15. In Winsnes, ed., *Artikler og taler,* pp. 27–34.
16. *Elleve aar,* p. 327.
17. *Fortellingen om Viga-Ljot og Vigdis,* Med. X, 48.
18. *Ibid.,* p. 52.
19. *Ibid.,* p. 139.
20. *Ibid.,* p. 164.
21. *Ibid.,* p. 161.

Chapter Three

1. *Jenny,* Mod. II, 208.
2. *Ibid.,* p. 84.
3. *Ibid.,* p. 191.
4. *Ibid.,* p. 203.
5. *Ibid.,* p. 204.
6. *Ibid.,* pp. 264–65.
7. *Ibid.,* p. 279.
8. *Ibid.,* p. 59.
9. "Nogen kvindesaksbetragtninger," first published in *Samtiden* (Oslo, 1912), p. 554; later included in *Et kvindesynspunkt,* 1919.
10. Anker, *op. cit.,* p. 20.
11. Winsnes, *Sigrid Undset,* p. 68.
12. *Elleve aar,* pp. 333, 335.
13. *Vaaren,* Mod. III, 10.
14. *Ibid.,* p. 189.
15. *Ibid.,* p. 25.

16. *Ibid.,* p. 70.
17. *Ibid.,* p. 106.
18. *Ibid.,* p. 118.
19. *Ibid.,* p. 182.
20. *Ibid.,* p. 209.
21. *Ibid.,* p. 245.
22. *Op. cit.,* p. 245.
23. First published in *Tidens tegn* (Oslo, 1919, Nos. 87, 88, 89); later included in *Et kvindesynspunkt.*
24. Introduction to "Efterskrift" ("Postscript"); later included in *Et kvindesynspunkt.*
25. *Splinten av troldspeilet,* Mod. IV, 108.
26. *Ibid.,* p. 109.
27. *Ibid.,* p. 123.
28. *Ibid.,* pp. 125–26.
29. Anker, *op. cit.,* p. 7.
30. *Gunnvald og Emma,* Mod. V, 82.

Chapter Four

1. "Sigrid Undset," in *Fem essays om moderne norsk litteratur* (Oslo, 1929), p. 7.
2. *Kransen* (*The Bridal Wreath*) and *Husfrue* (*The Mistress of Husaby*) have been dramatized by Tormod Skagestad. Metro-Goldwyn-Mayer has purchased the film rights to *Kristin Lavransdatter.*
3. Hamar, known as a seat of learning in the Middle Ages, became an episcopal see in 1152. Ruins of the twelfth-century cathedral are still standing.
4. *Kransen,* Med. I, 40.
5. *Ibid.,* p. 41.
6. *Ibid.,* p. 43.
7. *Ibid.,* p. 77.
8. *Ibid.,* p. 92.
9. *Ibid.,* p. 149.
10. *Ibid.,* p. 175.
11. *Ibid.,* p. 208.
12. *Ibid.,* p. 260.
13. *Ibid.,* p. 269.
14. Nidaros (Trondheim), founded in 997 by Olav Tryggvason, Christian king of Norway, was made an archiepiscopal see by Nicholas Breakspear (later Pope Adrian IV) in 1152. Christ Church, the finest Gothic cathedral in Scandinavia, was erected over the tomb of Olav Haraldsson (St. Olav) whose remains were laid to rest here after his death at the Battle of Stiklestad in 1030.

15. *Husfrue,* Med. II, 96.
16. *Ibid.,* p. 84.
17. *Ibid.,* p. 139.
18. *Ibid.,* Med. III, 146.
19. *Ibid.,* p. 167.
20. Winsnes, *Sigrid Undset,* p. 126.
21. *Korset,* Med. IV, 169.
22. *Ibid.,* p. 186.
23. *Ibid.,* pp. 188–89.
24. *Ibid.,* Med. V, 28.
25. In Norway it was considered an ill omen to give a son his father's name while the father was still living. Cf. also *Olav Audunssön i Hestviken,* Med. VI, 20: "In Norway no child is called after a living man—unless it be with the thought of putting him out of life."
26. *Korset,* Med. V, 44.
27. *Ibid.,* p. 86.
28. *Ibid.,* p. 200.
29. *Ibid.,* pp. 248–49.
30. *Husfrue,* Med. III, 67.
31. *Korset,* Med. IV, 51–52.
32. Cf. Chap. 1, note 39.
33. Cf. Chap. 1, note 38.
34. *Husfrue,* Med. III, 187.
35. Vinde, *op. cit.,* p. 35.
36. *Olav Audunssön i Hestviken,* Med. VI, 55.
37. *Ibid.,* p. 167.
38. *Ibid.,* pp. 169–70.
39. *Ibid.,* p. 182.
40. *Loc. cit.*
41. *Olav Audunssön i Hestviken,* Med. VII, 34–35.
42. *Ibid.,* p. 137.
43. *Ibid.,* p. 77.
44. *Ibid.,* p. 185.
45. *Ibid.,* p. 186.
46. *Ibid.,* p. 189.
47. *Olav Audunssön og hans börn,* Med. VIII, 43–44.
48. *Olav Audunssön og hans börn,* Med. IX, 296–97.
49. *Ibid.,* p. 305.
50. *Ibid.,* pp. 335–37.
51. Margaret Mary Dunn, "The Master of Hestviken: A New Reading," in *Scandinavian Studies* (1966 and 1968), Vol. 38, pp. 281–94, and Vol. 40, pp. 210–24.
52. *Olav Audunssön og hans börn,* Med. IX, 336–37.

53. Hanna Astrup Larsen, "Sigrid Undset," in *The American-Scandinavian Review* (New York, 1929), XVII, 13.

54. Winsnes, *Sigrid Undset*, pp. 151–52.

Chapter Five

1. *Gymnadenia*, Mod. VI, 67.
2. *Ibid.*, p. 94.
3. *Den brennende busk*, Mod. VII, 72.
4. *Gymnadenia*, Mod. VI, 209.
5. *Ibid.*, p. 85.
6. *Ibid.*, p. 212.
7. *Ibid.*, p. 206.
8. *Den brennende busk*, Mod. VII, 17–18.
9. *Ibid.*, p. 85.
10. Winsnes, *Sigrid Undset*, p. 176.
11. *Gymnadenia*, Mod. VI, 204–205.
12. N. Elizabeth Monroe, "Art and Ideas in Sigrid Undset," in *The Novel and Society*, p. 48.
13. Carl Nærup in *Tidens tegn* (Oslo, November 16, 1929).
14. *Den brennende busk*, Mod. VII, p. 344.
15. *Ida Elisabeth*, Mod. VIII, 144.
16. *Ibid.*, p. 142.
17. *Ibid.*, p. 260.
18. *Ibid.*, p. 305.
19. *Ibid.*, p. 352.
20. *Ibid.*, p. 365.
21. *Ibid.*, p. 382.
22. *Ibid.*, p. 388.
23. Gertrud von Le Fort, *Die Ewige Frau* (Munich, 1946), pp. 112–22.
24. *Ida Elisabeth*, Mod. VIII, 15.
25. *Ibid.*, p. 146.
26. Winsnes, *Sigrid Undset*, p. 200.
27. *Den trofaste hustru*, Mod. IX, 42.
28. *Ibid.*, p. 46.
29. *Ibid.*, p. 42.
30. *Ibid.*, p. 114.
31. *Ibid.*, p. 80.
32. *Loc. cit.*
33. *Ibid.*, p. 267.
34. *Ibid.*, p. 286.
35. *Ibid.*, pp. 286–87.
36. *Ibid.*, p. 297.

37. *Ibid.*, pp. 287–88.
38. *Ibid.*, p. 175.
39. Winsnes, *Sigrid Undset*, p. 208.
40. *Madame Dorthea*, Mod. X, 69.
41. *Ibid.*, p. 57.
42. *Ibid.*, pp. 154–55.
43. *Ibid.*, p. 166.
44. *Ibid.*, p. 262.
45. *Loc. cit.*
46. *Ibid.*, pp. 262–63.
47. *Ibid.*, p. 263.
48. *Ibid.*, p. 264.
49. *Loc. cit.*
50. *Tilbake til fremtiden*, p. 164.
51. *Ibid.*, p. 191.
52. *Ibid.*, p. 175.
53. *Ibid.*, p. 171.

Chapter Six

1. "Truth and Fiction," in *America* (New York, 1942), LXVII, 270.
2. *Loc. cit.*
3. Winsnes, *Sigrid Undset*, p. 247.
4. *Olav Audunssön i Hestviken*, Med. VII, 34–35.
5. *De sökte de gamle stier*, p. 93.

Selected Bibliography

A complete bibliography of Sigrid Undset literature has been compiled by Ida Packness in her *Sigrid Undset Bibliografi*, "Norsk Bibliografisk Bibliotek," Vol. 22. Oslo: Universitetsforlaget, 1963.

PRIMARY SOURCES

The most important of Sigrid Undset's works have been published by H. Aschehoug & Co. in Oslo. They appeared in twenty volumes (ten volumes of modern novels and ten volumes of medieval novels). The most recent editions have been used for this study. The complete set includes:

Romaner og Fortellinger fra Nutiden. Oslo: Aschehoug, 1964. Vols. I–X. (In this study the abbreviation Mod. is used to refer to these modern novels.)

  Vol. I. *Fru Marta Oulie. Den lykkelige alder.* 257 pp.
  Vol. II. *Jenny.* 306 pp.
  Vol. III. *Vaaren.* 282 pp.
  Vol. IV. *Splinten av troldspeilet. Vaarskyer.* 259 pp.
  Vol. V. *De kloge jomfruer. Fattige skjebner.* 307 pp.
  Vol. VI. *Gymnadenia.* 383 pp.
  Vol. VII. *Den brennende busk.* 439 pp.
  Vol. VIII. *Ida Elisabeth.* 389 pp.
  Vol. IX. *Den trofaste hustru.* 297 pp.
  Vol. X. *Madame Dorthea.* 266 pp.

Middelalderromaner. Oslo: Aschehoug, 1958. Vols. I–X. (In this study the abbreviation Med. is used for refer to these novels of the Middle Ages.)

  Vol. I. *Kristin Lavransdatter. Kransen.* 327 pp.
  Vols. II–III. *Kristin Lavransdatter. Husfrue.* 229 + 245 pp.
  Vols. IV–V. *Kristin Lavransdatter. Korset.* 242 + 250 pp.
  Vols. VI–VII. *Olav Audunssön i Hestviken.* 375 +285 pp.
  Vols. VIII–IX. *Olav Audunssön og hans börn.* 249 + 347 pp.
  Vol. X. *Fortellingen om Viga-Ljot og Vigdis og Sankt Halvards liv, död og jertegn.* 206 pp.

Other important works not included in this set are:

Et kvindesynspunkt. Oslo: Aschehoug, 1919. 177 pp.

Etapper. Ny række. Oslo: Aschehoug, 1933. 224 pp.

Elleve aar. Oslo: Aschehoug, 1934. 358 pp.

Selvportretter og landskapsbilleder. Oslo: Aschehoug, 1938. 247 pp.

Sigurd and His Brave Companions. A Tale of Medieval Norway.
(Originally written in German with the title: *Die Saga von
Vilmund Vidutan und seinen Gefährten.*) Illustrated by Gunvor
Bull Teilman. New York: Knopf, 1943. 139 pp. (Borzoi books for
young people.) Later translated into Norwegian by Signe Undset
Thomas as *Sigurd og hans tapre venner.* Oslo: Aschehoug, 1955.
190 pp.

True and Untrue and Other Norse Tales based on the original stories
from Asbjörnsen's and Moe's *folkeeventyr.* Edited and compiled
by Sigrid Undset. Illustrated by Frederick T. Chapman. New
York: Knopf, 1945. 253 pp.

Artikler og taler fra krigstiden. Edited by A. H. Winsnes. Oslo:
Aschehoug, 1952. 323 pp.

Quotations from Sigrid Undset's works are given in my own translation from the Norwegian texts. However, a list of published translations in English is added below. In referring to the author's works I
have also made use of these English titles.

TRANSLATIONS INTO ENGLISH

Jenny. Translated by W. Emmë. New York: Knopf, 1921.

Kristin Lavransdatter. The Bridal Wreath. Translated by Charles
Archer and J. S. Scott. New York: Knopf, 1923.—(*Kransen.*)

Kristin Lavransdatter. The Mistress of Husaby. Translated by Charles
Archer. New York: Knopf, 1925.—(*Husfrue.*)

Kristin Lavransdatter. The Cross. Translated by Charles Archer. New
York: Knopf, 1927.—(*Korset.*)

The Wild Orchid. Translated by Arthur G. Chater. New York: Knopf,
1931.—(*Gymnadenia.*)

The Burning Bush. Translated by Arthur G. Chater. New York: Knopf,
1932.—(*Den brennende busk.*)

Ida Elisabeth. Translated by Arthur G. Chater. New York: Knopf,
1933.

The Master of Hestviken. I. *The Axe;* II. *The Snake Pit;* III. *In the
Wilderness;* IV. *The Son Avenger.* Translated by Arthur G.
Chater. New York: Knopf, 1934.—(*Olav Audunssön i Hestviken*
and *Olav Audunssön og hans börn.*)

Stages on the Road. Translated by Arthur G. Chater. New York:
Knopf, 1934.—(*Etapper. Ny række.*)

Saga of Saints. Translated by E. C. Ramsden. New York: Longmans,
Green & Co., 1934.—(*Norske helgener.*)

The Longest Years. Translated by Arthur G. Chater. New York: Knopf, 1935.—(*Elleve aar.*)

Gunnar's Daughter. Translated by Arthur G. Chater. New York: Knopf, 1936.—(*Fortellingen om Viga-Ljot og Vigdis.*)

The Faithful Wife. Translated by Arthur G. Chater. New York: Knopf, 1937.—(*Den trofaste hustru.*)

Images in a Mirror. Translated by Arthur G. Chater. New York: Knopf, 1938.—(*Fru Hjelde* in *Splinten av troldspeilet.*)

Men, Women and Places. Translated by Arthur G. Chater. New York: Knopf, 1939.—(*Selvportretter og landskapsbilleder.*)

Madame Dorthea. Translated by Arthur G. Chater. New York: Knopf, 1940.

Return to the Future. Translated by Henriette C. K. Naeseth. New York: Knopf, 1942. (Borzoi books.)—(*Tilbake til fremtiden.*)

Happy Times in Norway. Translated by Joran Birkeland. New York: Knopf, 1942. (Borzoi books for young people.)—(*Lykkelige dager.*)

Four Stories. Translated by Naomi Walford. New York: Knopf, 1959. —(*Selma Bröter, Miss Smith-Tellefsen, Simonsen* from *Fattige skjebner,* and *Thjodolf* from *De kloge jomfruer.*)

BIOGRAPHICAL AND CRITICAL STUDIES

ANKER, NINI ROLL, *Min venn Sigrid Undset.* Oslo: Aschehoug, 1946.

BING, JUST, *Sigrid Undset.* Oslo: Aschehoug, 1924.

BÖÖK, FREDRIK, "Sigrid Undset," in *Från fyra sekler. Litterära essays.* Stockholm: Norstedt, 1928, pp. 198–244.

BRÖGGER, NIELS CHR., *Korset og rosen. En studie i Sigrid Undsets middelalder-diktning.* Oslo: Aschehoug, 1952.

DESCHAMPS, NICOLE, *Sigrid Undset ou la Morale de la Passion.* Montreal: University of Montreal Press, 1966.

DE VOS, A. M. F., *Sigrid Undset.* Ghent: Piet Schepens, 1953.

DUNN, MARGARET MARY, "The Master of Hestviken: A New Reading," in *Scandinavian Studies* (1966), pp. 281–94 and (1968), pp. 210–24.

ENGELSTAD, CARL FREDRIK, *Mennesker og makter. Sigrid Undsets middelalderromaner.* Oslo: Aschehoug, 1940.

GUSTAFSON, ALRIK, "Christian Ethics in a Pagan World: Sigrid Undset," in *Six Scandinavian Novelists.* Minneapolis: University of Minnesota Press, [1968], pp. 286–361.

HASLUND, EBBA, *Sigrid Undset. Kristin Lavransdatter:* 1. *Kransen,* 2. *Husfrue,* 3. *Korset.* A Student's Handbook prepared for Norsk Korrespondanseskole. Oslo, 1959.

HAAKONSEN, DANIEL, "Om pakt-begrepet i *Kristin Lavransdatter,*" in *Tradisjon og fornyelse* (Oslo, 1959), pp. 260–71.

KIELLAND, EUGENIA, "Sigrid Undset," in *Fem essays om moderne norsk litteratur*. Oslo: Aschehoug, 1929, pp. 7–41.

LARSEN, HANNA ASTRUP, "Sigrid Undset," in *The American-Scandinavian Review* (New York, 1929), pp. 344–52 and 406–14.

MARBLE, ANNIE RUSSELL, "Sigrid Undset: Novelist of Medieval Norway," in *The Nobel Prize Winners in Literature 1901–1931*.

MOEN, HANNE HELLIESEN, *Opplysninger til Sigrid Undsets Middelalderromaner*. Oslo: Aschehoug, 1950.

MONROE, N. ELIZABETH, "Art and Idea in Sigrid Undset," in *The Novel and Society*. Chapel Hill: University of North Carolina Press, 1941, pp. 39–87.

PAASCHE, FREDRIK, "Sigrid Undset og norsk middelalder," in *Samtiden* (Oslo, 1929), pp. 1–12.

RIEBER-MOHN, HALLVARD, "Om gudsbegrepet hos Sigrid Undset," in *Samtiden* (Oslo, 1955), pp. 462–74.

RUCH, VELMA N., *Sigrid Undset's "Kristin Lavransdatter": A Study of its Literary Art and its Reception in America, England and Scandinavia*. Unpublished dissertation, University of Wisconsin, 1957.

SKOUEN, ARNE, "Sigrid Undset i Amerika," in *Samtiden* (Oslo, 1947), pp. 323–32.

VINDE, VICTOR, *Sigrid Undset. A Nordic Moralist*. Translated from French into English by Babette and Glenn Hughes. Seattle: University of Washington Press, 1930.

VON LE FORT, GERTRUD, *Die Ewige Frau*. Munich: Kösel-Pustet, 1946.

WINSNES, A. H., *Sigrid Undset: En studie i kristen realisme*. Oslo: Aschehoug, 1949. Translated into English by P. G. Foote, *Sigrid Undset: A Study in Christian Realism*. London and New York: Sheed & Ward, 1953. I have quoted from Foote's English translation.

Index

A. Personal Names